THE AGE OF EXPLORATION

FROM CHRISTOPHER COLUMBUS TO FERDINAND MAGELLAN

THE AGE OF EXPLORATION

FROM CHRISTOPHER COLUMBUS TO FERDINAND MAGELLAN

EDITED BY KENNETH PLETCHER, SENIOR EDITOR, GEOGRAPHY

Britannica
Educational Publishing

IN ASSOCIATION WITH

ROSEN
EDUCATIONAL SERVICES

Published in 2014 by Britannica Educational Publishing
(a trademark of Encyclopædia Britannica, Inc.) in association with Rosen Educational Services, LLC
29 East 21st Street, New York, NY 10010.

Distributed exclusively by Rosen Educational Services.
For a listing of additional Britannica Educational Publishing titles, call toll free (800) 237-9932.

First Edition

Britannica Educational Publishing
J.E. Luebering: Director, Core Reference Group
Adam Augustyn: Assistant Manager, Core Reference Group
Marilyn L. Barton: Senior Coordinator, Production Control
Steven Bosco: Director, Editorial Technologies
Lisa S. Braucher: Senior Producer and Data Editor
Yvette Charboneau: Senior Copy Editor
Kathy Nakamura: Manager, Media Acquisition
Kenneth Pletcher, Senior Editor, Geography

Rosen Educational Services
Shalini Saxena: Editor
Nelson Sá: Art Director
Cindy Reiman: Photography Manager
Amy Feinberg: Photo Researcher
Brian Garvey: Designer, Cover Design
Introduction by Kenneth Pletcher

Library of Congress Cataloging-in-Publication Data

The age of exploration: from Christopher Columbus to Ferdinand Magellan/edited by
Kenneth Pletcher.—1st ed.
    p. cm.—(The Britannica guide to explorers and adventurers)
Includes bibliographical references and index.
ISBN 978-1-62275-019-1 (library binding)
1. Discoveries in geography. 2. Explorers. I. Pletcher, Kenneth.
G200.A37 2013
910.92'2—dc23

2012038340

Manufactured in the United States of America

On the cover: A ship whose design is typical of those employed during the Age of
Exploration. *iurii/Shutterstock.com*

Cover, p. iii (ornamental graphic) istockphoto.com/Angelgild; interior pages (scroll) istock-
photo.com/U.P. Images, (background texture) istockphoto.com/Peter Zelei

CONTENTS

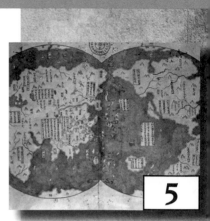

5

7

21

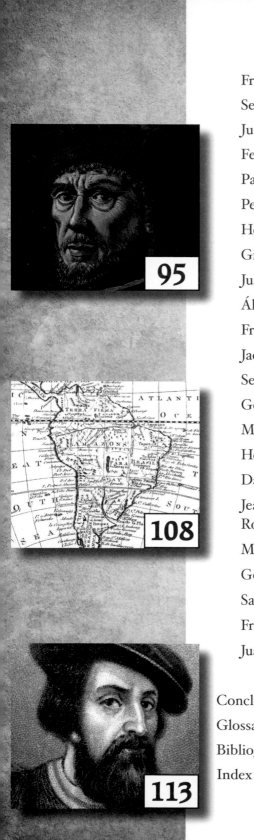

INTRODUCTION

The century and a half between 1400 and 1550 was a remarkable time in world history. In Asia, the continent's two great civilizations, China and India, were developing highly sophisticated cultures—the Chinese under the Ming dynasty (1368–1644) and India under a series of smaller polities that eventually became the Mughal empire (early 16th–mid-18th century). In both lands, especially in China, much of the external focus during that time was on preventing more of the incursions from Mongols that had so dominated previous centuries. Indeed, perhaps the most enduring legacy of the Ming is China's Great Wall, the remaining sections of which are testament to the enormous resources the Chinese expended maintaining and expanding that barrier and symbolic of their efforts to keep outsiders at bay.

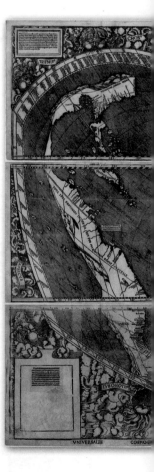

Meanwhile, throughout Europe, nations centred on monarchies were beginning to emerge from the manor-based decentralized feudal society that had been in place for centuries. The process progressed to such a degree that by the beginning of the 16th century, centralized authority, within the frontiers of the nation-state, covered much of the continent—the first time it had been so since the Roman Empire. The economy of Europe was also being transformed from one largely of labour services provided to lords by the serf class to more of a money economy in which peasants, artisans, and merchants played an increasing role. This was made possible in large part by the terrible plague epidemics of the second half of the 14th century, which had so depleted the continent's population that they had contributed significantly to the ruin of the landowners.

The 15th and 16th centuries also witnessed the great cultural and intellectual flowering in Europe known as

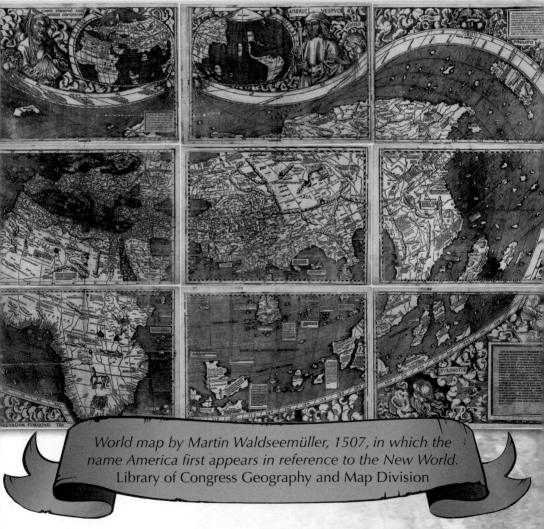

World map by Martin Waldseemüller, 1507, in which the name America first appears in reference to the New World. Library of Congress Geography and Map Division

the Renaissance that produced such renowned individuals as Leonardo da Vinci, Niccolò Machiavelli, and William Shakespeare, as well as the remarkable innovation of printing with movable type that greatly facilitated the dissemination of information. While much of Asia may have been focused more inward than outward during that time, Europe was looking to push beyond its boundaries, drawn by the wonders and riches of the East that it had learned of from such travelers as Marco Polo. Access to the East by land, however, had become difficult by 1400. The vast empire of the Mongols, which had once stretched across Eurasia, was much diminished, and European merchants could no longer rely on the safety of such land routes as the ancient Silk Road. In addition, the Ottoman Turks, who were hostile to Christian Europeans, were growing in power in the Middle East, and they effectively blocked the outlets to the Mediterranean Sea of Europe's traditional sea routes from Asia.

Those circumstances, along with the growing desire of the emerging European states for trade and adventure, became great incentives for those in the West to seek new sea routes to Asia. The first great overseas voyages of the 15th century, however, did not originate in the West but were those of the renowned Chinese admiral Zheng He, sent by the Ming on seven expeditions between 1405 and 1433. That would prove to be the last such venture mounted by the East. In contrast, in the 100 years between the mid-15th and the mid-16th century, a seemingly endless stream of explorers and adventurers struck out from European shores.

The first of these remarkable European enterprises was the search for a southern sea route to China, initiated by Prince Henry the Navigator of Portugal, who sent out a series of expeditions to explore the Atlantic coast of Africa. By the time of his death, in 1460, his captains had reached as far south as what is now Sierra Leone. The

Portuguese continued pushing farther south and east along the coast, until Bartolomeu Dias (or Diaz) rounded the Cape of Good Hope in 1488 and proved the existence of an open sea passage between the Atlantic and Indian oceans. By the end of the century, Vasco da Gama had led the voyage around the Cape that reached the west coast of India and provided the final western link in the route to China.

In 1500 yet another Portuguese fleet set out for India, this one under the command of Pedro Alvarez Cabral. He had been advised to sail southwestward to avoid the calm waters off the coast of Guinea, but he sailed so far to the west that he reached Brazil. Initial enthusiasm for this discovery soon waned, however, as Portugal maintained its eastward focus. Trading entrepôts were quickly established along the African coast, at strategic entrances to the Red Sea and the Persian Gulf, and at locations such as Goa along the coast of the Indian subcontinent. By 1512 Portugal had established a base on the Strait of Malacca— and thus could control access to the South China Sea—and had reached the Spice Islands (Moluccas) and the island of Java (both now parts of Indonesia).

While the Portuguese were sailing ever eastward and then establishing their trading outposts, the Genoese navigator Christopher Columbus was trying to convince the king and queen of Spain that he could reach the East by traveling west. This was still an audacious notion at the end of the 15th century, even though many believed by then that a western route was possible. Columbus did get royal backing, and in August 1492 set forth with a fleet of three small ships. The party made landfall two months later, believing they had reached "Cipango" (Japan), when, in fact they had encountered a small island in what is now the Lesser Antilles archipelago in the Caribbean. More lands were explored in the Caribbean and Gulf of

Mexico region during Columbus' subsequent voyages in the region, but it was not clear yet that this was an entirely new land and not Asia.

By the end of the 15th century, during the latter years of Columbus' activities in the new lands, another Italian-born navigator, John Cabot, was exploring part of the northeastern coast of North America for Britain. Yet another Italian, Amerigo Vespucci, who was a friend of Columbus, took part in two extensive voyages (1499–1500 and 1501–02) along the coast of South America. In the years following his return, Vespucci and scholars became convinced that all who had sailed westward had discovered a New World. This land soon came to be called America, named for the intrepid navigator. Nonetheless, although it soon was widely accepted that the Americas were not part of the Old World, vestiges of the earlier notion persisted and survive to this day: the indigenous peoples of these lands are still called "Indians," and the islands of the Caribbean are the West Indies—the counterpart to the true (East) Indies now known as Indonesia.

After 1500, increasing numbers of Europeans reached the eastern shores of the Americas and began pushing inland. The Spaniard Juan Ponce de Léon, founder of the first colony on Puerto Rico, discovered and explored Florida (1513), and, in that same year, Vasco Núñez de Balboa became the first European to view the Pacific Ocean from America. Surveys of the coast of the Yucatán Peninsula, sent out by Diego Velázquez de Cuéllar, governor of Cuba, paved the way for the overland expedition (1519–21) of conquistador Hernán Cortés that led to the Spanish conquest of Mexico and the Aztec Empire. Over the next several years following the establishment of Spanish authority in Mexico, the west coast of South America was explored by Spaniards Diego de Almagro and Francisco Pizarro, during which time they discovered

Peru and encountered the Inca. Pizzaro subsequently spearheaded the subjugation of the Inca and founded the city of Lima.

A number of other Spaniards engaged in significant but perhaps somewhat less recognized exploits during the first half of the 16th century. Among the most remarkable of these was Francisco de Orellana. He not only brought back stories of riches and wondrous lands, but made a pioneering journey down the Amazon River (1541–42) and coined the river's name. Hernando (or Fernando) de Soto explored southeastern North America and discovered the Mississippi River (1537–42), though he did not survive the ordeal. Francisco Vázquez de Coronado led expeditions in southwestern North America (1540–42) that failed to find the fabled Seven Golden Cities of Cibola but did discover the great wonder of the Grand Canyon. Finally, Juan Rodríguez Cabrillo, reputed to be a conquistador of Central America, is believed to have been the first European to explore the Pacific coast of California (1542).

While the Spanish were working to acquire and then consolidate the vast territory that came to be called New Spain, they also were still seeking what they hoped would be an easy way through the barrier of the Americas to the wealth of Asia. They were to find, however, that not only would the route be difficult, but that once the barrier was passed, Asia would be a far greater distance away than they had imagined. The Portuguese navigator Ferdinand Magellan was selected by Spain to lead the expedition that would find this western route. After leaving Spain in 1519, Magellan's small fleet sailed down the coast of South America before discovering and passing through the strait that now bears his name and then beginning the long perilous journey across the Pacific. Magellan was killed in the Philippines, and only one of his remaining ships finally reached Spain three years after it had departed. Still, one of the most extraordinary feats of navigation had been accomplished, and the extent of the globe had been established.

Meanwhile, the French and, to some extent, the British were beginning the exploration of northern North America. John Cabot's son Sebastian undertook expeditions for Britain as well as Spain. In the 1520s the Italian navigator Giovanni de Verrazzano explored the east coast of what would become the United States, becoming the first European to sight the New York City region. The French mariner Jacques Cartier led several explorations of the Canadian coast and St. Lawrence River between 1534 and 1542, and these became the basis of the French claims in North America. Cartier was followed to the region by Jean-François de La Rocque, sieur (lord) de Roberval, who in 1542–43 attempted unsuccessfully to found the first French colony at what is now Quebec city. After this failure, the French made no effort to establish another colony in northeastern North America until the beginning of the 17th century.

Often accompanying the conquistadores and other explorer-colonists were priests and missionaries, a small number of whom were more adventuresome than the others and made their marks as explorers. One of these, the Franciscan friar Marcos de Niza, led an expedition across what is now the southwestern United States and claimed to have sighted the Seven Cities that Coronado tried in vain to find. Without a doubt, however, St. Francis Xavier was the most remarkable of these emissaries. He was one of Jesuit founder Ignatius of Loyola's original disciples, and, over a period of about a decade (1542–52), he established Christianity in India, the Malay Archipelago, and Japan.

By 1550 the Age of Exploration was largely over. True, there were vast regions of land and sea that remained unknown, and new waves of explorers and adventurers were poised to undertake those journeys of discovery. But most of the truly pioneering and seminal voyages had been made by then, and the true dimensions and size of our world were basically understood. That world—with broad, seemingly endless seas, vast unexpected and largely unpopulated landmasses, and new peoples and cultures wholly unlike any previously encountered—was substantially different from the notion people had had of it 150 years earlier. This volume recounts the extraordinary stories of those who ventured out into this unexplored world at great peril, many not surviving to return. Often driven by the lure of riches and fame as well as the excitement of discovery, they risked their lives and the lives of those whom they commanded as they sailed into the unknown. One marvels at the sheer audacity of these undertakings, with explorers embarking as they did on these world-changing ventures with only the simplest charts and navigational tools. Perhaps the only comparison there can be to them in this day and age are the brave souls who ventured to the Moon and back in the 1960s and '70s.

ZHENG HE

(b. c. 1371, Kunyang [in present-day Jinning county], Yunnan province, China—d. 1433, Calicut [now Kozhikode], India)

The Chinese admiral and diplomat Zheng He (or Chang Ho) undertook several long sea voyages and helped to extend Chinese maritime and commercial influence throughout the regions bordering the Indian Ocean. A Muslim, he was born Ma Sanbao (later Ma He) the son of a ḥājjī (a Muslim who had made the pilgrimage to Mecca). His family claimed descent from an early Mongol governor of Yunnan province in southwestern China as well as from King Muḥammad of Bukhara. The family name Ma was derived from the Chinese rendition of Muḥammad. In 1381, when he was about 10 years old, Yunnan, the last Mongol hold in China, was reconquered by Chinese forces led by generals of the newly established Ming dynasty. The young Ma was among the boys who were captured, castrated, and sent into the army as orderlies. By 1390, when these troops were placed under the command of the prince of Yan, Ma He had distinguished himself as a junior officer, skilled in war and diplomacy; he also made influential friends at court.

In 1400 the prince of Yan revolted against his nephew, the Jianwen emperor, taking the throne in 1402 as the Yongle emperor. Under the Yongle administration (1402–24), the war-devastated economy of China was soon

Illustration of Zheng He, appearing in a fictional account of his voyages. HIP/Art Resource, NY

restored. The Ming court then sought to display its naval power to bring the maritime states of South and Southeast Asia in line.

For 300 years the Chinese had been extending their power out to sea. An extensive seaborne commerce had developed to meet the taste of the Chinese for spices and aromatics and the need for raw industrial materials. Chinese travelers abroad, as well as Indian and Muslim visitors, widened the geographic horizon of the Chinese. Technological developments in shipbuilding and in the arts of seafaring reached new heights by the beginning of the Ming.

The emperor had conferred on Ma He (who had become a court eunuch of great influence) the surname Zheng, and he was thenceforth known as Zheng He. Selected by the emperor to be commander in chief of the missions to the "Western Oceans," he first set sail in 1405, commanding 62 ships and 27,800 men. The fleet visited Champa (now in southern Vietnam), Siam (Thailand), Malacca (Melaka), and Java; then through the Indian Ocean to Calicut (Kozhikode) and Ceylon (Sri Lanka). Zheng He returned to China in 1407.

On his second voyage, in 1408–09, Zheng He again visited Calicut—stopping as well in Chochin (Kochi) to the south—but encountered treachery from King Alagonakkara of Ceylon. Zheng defeated his forces and took the king back to Nanjing as a captive. In October 1409 Zheng He set out on his third voyage. This time, going beyond the seaports of India, he sailed to Hormuz on the Persian Gulf. On his return in 1411 he touched at Samudra, on the northern tip of Sumatra.

Zheng He left China in 1413 on his fourth voyage. After stopping at the principal ports of Asia, he proceeded westward from India to Hormuz. A detachment of the fleet cruised southward down the Arabian coast, visiting Djofar and Aden. A Chinese mission visited Mecca and continued to Egypt. The fleet visited Brava and Malindi and almost reached the Mozambique Channel. On his return to China in 1415, Zheng He brought the envoys of more than 30 states of South and Southeast Asia to pay homage to the Chinese emperor.

During Zheng He's fifth voyage (1417–19), the Ming fleet revisited the Persian Gulf and the east coast of Africa. A sixth voyage was launched in 1421 to take home the foreign emissaries from China. Again he visited Southeast Asia, India, Arabia, and Africa. In 1424 the Yongle emperor died. His successor, the Hongxi emperor, suspended naval expeditions abroad in a shift of policy. Zheng He was appointed garrison commander in Nanjing, with the task of disbanding his troops.

Zheng He's seventh and final voyage left China in the winter of 1431, visiting the states of Southeast Asia, the coast of India, the Persian Gulf, the Red Sea, and the east coast of Africa. He died in Calicut in the spring of 1433, and the fleet returned to China that summer.

Zheng He was the best known of the Yongle emperor's diplomatic agents. Although some historians see no achievement in the naval expeditions other than flattering the emperor's vanity, these missions did have the effect of extending China's political sway over maritime Asia for half a century. Admittedly, they did not, like similar voyages of European merchant-adventurers, lead to the establishment of trading empires. Yet, in their wake, Chinese emigration increased, resulting in Chinese colonization in Southeast Asia and the accompanying tributary trade, which lasted to the 19th century.

Copy of a world map that some believe reflects the voyages of Zheng He. Although it renewed interest in Zheng He's expeditions since its discovery in 2005, the map has been largely discredited by experts. Universal Images Group/Getty Images

PRINCE HENRY THE NAVIGATOR

(b. March 4, 1394, Porto, Portugal—d.
November 13, 1460, Vila do Infante, near
Sagres)

The Portuguese nobleman Prince Henry the Navigator (Portuguese: Henrique o Navegador) is noted for the impetus and sponsorship he gave to maritime exploration—especially the voyages of discovery along the western coast of Africa—that led to the great expansion of Europe in the 16th century. The epithet Navigator, applied to him by the English (though seldom by Portuguese writers), is a misnomer, as he himself never embarked on any exploratory voyages. His enduring importance thus has been as a legendary figure of the early stages of European exploration and discovery, as well as an exemplar of Portuguese nationalism.

EARLY CAREER

Henry—his full name, in Portuguese, was Henrique, *infante* (prince) de Portugal, *duque* (duke) de Viseu, *senhor* (lord) da Covilhã—was the third son of King John I and Philippa of Lancaster, the daughter of John of Gaunt of England. Henry and his older brothers, the princes Duarte (Edward) and Pedro, were educated under the supervision of their parents. Henry emerged with pronounced tastes for chivalric romance and astrological literature, as well as

Prince Henry the Navigator.
Danita Delimont/Gallo Images/Getty Images

with ambitions to take part in military campaigns and, if possible, win a kingdom for himself.

The starting point of Henry's career was the capture of the Moroccan city of Ceuta in 1415. According to Henry's enthusiastic biographer, Gomes Eanes de Zurara, the three princes persuaded their still-vigorous father to undertake a campaign that would enable them to win their knightly spurs in genuine combat instead of in the mock warfare of a tournament. King John consented and, with Ceuta in mind, began military preparations, meanwhile spreading rumours of another destination, in order to lull the Moroccan city into a feeling of false security.

Although a plague swept Portugal and claimed the queen as a victim, the army sailed in July 1415. King John found Ceuta unprepared, as he had hoped, and its capture unexpectedly easy. Though Zurara later claimed the principal role in the victory for Henry, it would seem that the experienced soldier-king actually directed the operation. That Henry distinguished himself, however, is indicated by his immediate appointment as the king's lieutenant for Ceuta; the position did not require his permanent residence there or confer civil authority or administrative responsibilities but did oblige him to see that the city was adequately defended.

An emergency arose in 1418, when the Muslim rulers of Fez (Fès) in Morocco and the kingdom of Granada in Spain joined in an attempt to retake the city. Henry hastened to the rescue with reinforcements but on arrival found that the Portuguese garrison had beaten off the assailants. He then proposed to attack Granada, despite reminders that this would antagonize the kingdom of Castile, on whose threshold it lay. But his father, who had spent years fighting the attempts of the Castilians to annex Portugal, wanted peace with them and sent peremptory orders to return home.

On his return to Portugal, Henry was made duke of Viseu and lord of Covilhã. In 1420, at the age of 26, he was made administrator general of the Order of Christ, which had replaced the crusading order of the Templars in Portugal. While this did not oblige him to take religious vows, it was reported that he afterward resolved to lead a chaste and ascetic life. However, the traditional view of Henry as indifferent to all but religion and the furtherance of his mission of discovery is not supported by later scholarship. Indeed, Henry had not always refrained from worldly pleasures; as a young man he had fathered an illegitimate daughter. Moreover, his brother Duarte, especially after becoming king, did not hesitate to lecture and reprove Henry for such shortcomings as extravagance, immethodical habits, failure to keep promises, and lack of scruples in the raising of money.

PATRONAGE OF EXPLORATORY EXPEDITIONS

Funds appropriated from the Order of Christ largely financed the Atlantic voyages along the western coast of Africa that Henry began to promote in the mid-1420s. He sought opportunities to take part in the commerce of traditional West African products, especially slaves and gold, and to establish potentially profitable colonies on under-exploited islands, the most successful of which he helped to found on Madeira.

Henry's interest in geography unquestionably was influenced by the travels of Prince Pedro, his older and perhaps more brilliant brother. In 1425 Pedro set out on a long tour of Europe on which he visited England, Flanders, Germany, Hungary, and the principalities of Moldavia and Walachia (now Romania) before returning home through Italy, Aragon, and Castile. In eastern Europe he was close enough to Ottoman Turkey to appreciate the Muslim danger. From Italy Pedro brought home to Portugal, in 1428, a copy of Marco Polo's travels that he had translated for Prince Henry's benefit.

Henry's other older brother, Duarte, succeeded King John in 1433. During the five years of Duarte's reign, lack of success in the Canary Islands induced Henry's captains to venture farther down the Atlantic coast of Africa in search of other opportunities. Tradition has claimed that the most important achievement was the rounding of Cape Bojador in 1434 by Gil Eanes, who overcame a superstition that had previously deterred seamen. It seems, however, that this is at best an exaggeration, resulting from the vagueness of the sailing directions reported in Portuguese sources. What Eanes mistakenly called Cape Bojador was actually Cape Juby, which had already been passed by many earlier navigators. During the next years, Henry's captains pushed southward somewhat beyond the Rio de Oro. They also began the colonization of the recently discovered Azores, through the orders of both Henry and Pedro.

In 1437 Henry and his younger brother, Fernando, gained Duarte's reluctant consent for an expedition against Tangier. Ceuta had proved an economic liability, and they believed that possession of the neighbouring city would both ensure Ceuta's safety and provide a source of revenue. Pedro opposed the undertaking. Henry and Fernando nevertheless attacked Tangier and met with disaster; Henry had shown poor generalship and mismanaged the enterprise. The Portuguese army would have been unable to reembark had not Fernando been left as hostage in exchange for Henry's broken promise to surrender Ceuta. Fernando's death at Fez in 1443 seems to have been felt by Henry as a grave charge upon his conscience.

King Duarte died in 1438, shortly before Henry's return. His heir, Afonso V, was only six at the time, and Pedro assumed the regency over the bitter opposition of the boy's mother, Leonor of Aragon, who would willingly have accepted Henry as regent. Nevertheless, for most of the next decade Pedro and Henry worked in harmony.

In 1441 a caravel returned from the West African coast with some gold dust and slaves, thus silencing the growing criticism that Henry was wasting money on a profitless enterprise. One of Henry's voyagers, Dinís Dias, in 1445 reached the mouth of the Sénégal River (then taken for a branch of the Nile); and a year later Nuño Tristão, another of Henry's captains, sighted the Gambia River. By 1448 the trade in slaves to Portugal had become sufficiently extensive for Henry to order the building of a fort and warehouse on Arguin Island.

Afonso V attained his legal majority at the age of 14 in 1446. His embittered mother had meanwhile died in Castile, and although the young king presently married Pedro's daughter, Isabel, Pedro turned full power over to the youth with obvious reluctance.

Armed conflict between the two became inevitable, and Henry in the end felt obliged to side with the king, though he remained as much as possible in the background. He took no part in a skirmish at Alfarrobeira in May 1449, in which Pedro was killed by a chance shot from a crossbowman. Henry's biographer, Zurara, on the other hand, declared that his hero did everything possible to prevent Pedro's death and promised to explain the circumstances further in later writings; but if he did so, the account is lost.

FINAL VENTURES

After Alfarrobeira, Henry spent most of his time at Sagres, his castle in the far south of Portugal. He was accorded

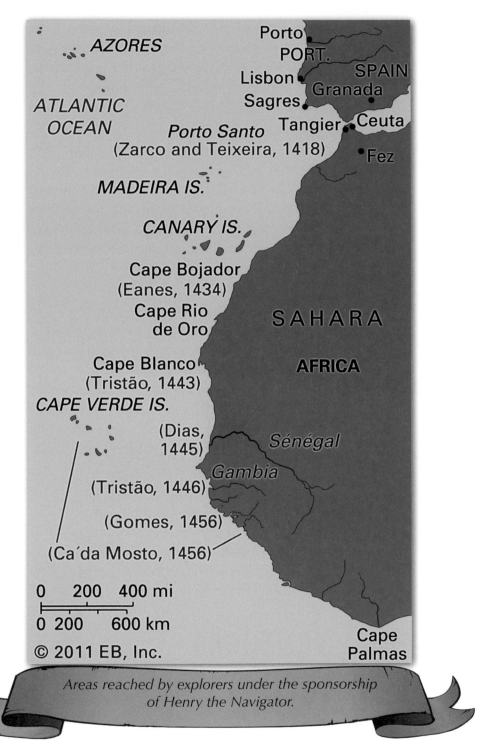

Areas reached by explorers under the sponsorship of Henry the Navigator.

by the king the sole right to send ships to visit and trade with the Guinea coast of Africa. He appeared occasionally at the Lisbon court and in 1450 helped arrange for the marriage of the King's sister to the emperor Frederick III. During most of his last decade, Henry concentrated on the sponsorship of voyages. These accomplished only minor discoveries, as the prince now seemed mainly interested in exploiting resources—especially African slaves and, from 1452, the sugar of Madeira—in the regions already contacted. The last two important mariners sent out by Henry were the Venetian explorer Alvise Ca' da Mosto and the Portuguese Diogo Gomes, who between them discovered several of the Cape Verde Islands.

Afonso V had small interest in discovery but great zeal for crusading and knight-errantry. Resuming the old attempt at Moroccan conquest, he led an expedition in 1458 against Alcácer Ceguer (now Ksar es-Shrhir), in which Henry accompanied him. The prince, now 64, did well in the fighting, and, when the town capitulated, Afonso left the surrender terms to his uncle, who showed remarkable leniency. Henry lived for two years after his return from Alcácer Ceguer.

EVALUATION

The farthest point south that was reached during Henry's lifetime was probably present-day Sierra Leone; after his death, the pace of progress in Portuguese exploration accelerated markedly, suggesting that the prince's reputation as a patron of explorers has been exaggerated. Although the colonization of Madeira proved, at least for a while, to be a brilliant success, most of his enterprises failed. The Canary Islands, the focus of his most unremitting obsessions, eventually fell to Spain, and Portugal did not succeed in garnering much of the African gold trade until more than 20 years after the prince's death. His desire to convert the peoples of the Canary Islands and West Africa to Christianity was often voiced but was largely unsupported by action. Nor is Henry's traditional reputation as a champion of the advancement of science supported by any genuine evidence. He did, however, commission chronicles by Zurara that presented a heroic image of himself—an image that has persisted to the present day.

NICCOLÒ DEI CONTI

(b. c. 1395, Chioggia?, near Venice [Italy]—d. 1469, Venice?)

Niccolò dei Conti was a Venetian merchant who brought back a vivid account of his 25 years of travels in southern Asia. As a young man living in Damascus, he learned Arabic. In 1414 he set out for Baghdad, then journeyed down the Tigris River and eventually reached Hormuz (now in Iran), near the southern end of the Persian Gulf. He moved on to Calacatia, a trading centre on the Persian coast, learned the language, and entered a partnership with some Persian merchants who accompanied him on his travels.

In India, where he apparently married an Indian woman, he visited the state of Cambay in the northwest; Vijayanagar (now Hampi, Karnataka state), about 150 miles (240 km) east of Goa; and Maliapur (now Mylapore, a suburb of modern Chennai [Madras]). Maliapur, regarded as the resting place of St. Thomas the Apostle, was the shrine most sacred to Indian Christians. He then went to Sumatra, where he encountered cannibalism and found pepper and gold. He also visited Tenasserim, now in Myanmar (Burma), and the Ganges River delta region. In Myanmar he sailed down the Irrawaddy River, stopping at the prosperous city of Pegu.

Java was the farthest point Conti reached. By way of Ciampa (perhaps modern Thailand) and probably Ceylon (now Sri Lanka), he went on to Quilon in extreme southwestern India. His stops along India's Malabar Coast included Cochin (now Kochi) and Calicut (now Kozhikode). He revisited Cambay before making his way to the southern coast of the Arabian Peninsula and the city of Aden. He also stopped at Jidda, the port for Mecca, and then went overland to Cairo and Mt. Sinai before arriving in Venice (1444). As penance for renouncing Christianity during his travels he was required to recount his ventures to Pope Eugenius IV's secretary, the scholar and humanist Poggio (Gian Francesco Poggio Bracciolini). His narrative, recorded in Latin, is a valuable account of southern Asia in the 15th century. It appeared in 1857 in an English translation, edited by R.H. Major, as India in the fifteenth century.

DINÍS DIAS

(fl. 15th century)

The Portuguese navigator and explorer Dinís Dias was one of the maritime explorers whom Prince Henry the Navigator sent to expand Portugal's knowledge of the northern and western Atlantic coasts of Africa. As captain of a caravel in 1445, Dias sailed as captain of one such expedition in 1445 past the outflowing mouth of the Sénégal River. Dias subsequently discovered Cape Verde, the westernmost point of Africa. He chose that name— meaning "Green Cape"—because the headland had tall trees and fragrant vegetation. Dias and his crew were repulsed by the local peoples when they tried to land and soon returned to Portugal.

In 1446 Prince Henry formed a fleet of caravels that were to show the Portuguese flag along the African coast and explore the Sénégal River, which the Portuguese at the time believed was the western branch of the Nile. Dias commanded one of the vessels.

ALVISE CA' DA MOSTO

(b. 1432, Venice [Italy]—d. July 18, 1488, Venice)

Alvise Ca' da Mosto (or Cadamosto) was a Venetian traveler and nobleman who wrote one of the earliest known accounts of western Africa.

In 1454 Ca' da Mosto obtained permission from Prince Henry the Navigator to make a voyage to the south along the African coast. He set sail on March 22, 1455, accompanied by Italian explorer Antoniotto Usodimare. He visited Madeira and the Canary Islands, and coasted along the western Sahara to past the mouth of the Sénégal River, which had been reached earlier by Portuguese navigators. Ca' da Mosto ascended some distance up the Gambia

River, but, finding the people living there hostile, he returned to Portugal.

Ca' da Mosto's company appears to have been the first European expedition to reach the Cape Verde Islands, two of which he explored (1456) and found uninhabited. Returning to the African shore, he sailed south from the region of the Gambia to the coast of present-day Guinea-Bissau. His account of the voyage contains a thorough study of Senegambian ethnography and slavery. He is credited with creating a portolan chart—a chart of sailing directions—for the Mediterranean that was later widely used by Italian navigators. Ca' da Mosto returned to Portugal in 1463, where he subsequently held important official appointments.

Martín Alonso and Vicente Yáñez Pinzón

(b. c. 1441, Palos de Moguer, Sevilla [Spain]—d. 1493, Palos de Moguer), (b. c. 1460?, Palos de Moguer—d. c. 1523)

The two brothers Martín Alonso and Vicente Yáñez Pinzón were from a family of Spanish shipowners and navigators who took part in Christopher Columbus' first voyage to America.

Martín, part owner of the *Pinta* and *Niña*—two of the three vessels used on the voyage—helped prepare them, procured crews for the expedition of 1492, and commanded the *Pinta*, on which his brother Francisco was pilot. His suggestion to change course on October 7 brought the fleet to a landfall in the Bahamas on October 12. Near Cuba, however, he left the fleet to search for the land of gold and spices. He rejoined Columbus a few months later but, returning to Spain, became separated from the main fleet and died only a few weeks after his arrival.

Vicente commanded the *Niña* in 1492–93 and remained with Columbus throughout the expedition. A successful and capable explorer in his own right, he sailed in late 1499 and landed on the Brazilian coast at a cape he named Santa María de la Consolación. From there, sailing northwest, he reached and explored the Amazon River estuary before continuing to the Gulf of Paria (northeastern Venezuela). He made two additional voyages to the New World before 1508. In that year, having been commissioned to discover a passage to the Spice Islands, he sailed with Juan Díaz de Solís and may have seen the coasts of what are now Honduras and the Yucatán (Mexico).

FRANCISCO DE ALMEIDA

(b. c. 1450, Lisbon, Portugal—d. March 1, 1510,
Table Bay [modern Cape Town, South Africa])

The soldier and explorer Francisco de Almeida was the first viceroy of Portuguese India.

After Almeida had achieved fame in the wars against the Moors, the Portuguese king Manuel I made him viceroy of the newly conquered territories of India in March 1505. Setting forth with a powerful fleet of 21 ships, he rounded the Cape of Good Hope and, sailing up Africa's east coast, took Kilwa (in what is now Tanzania), where he constructed a fort, and then destroyed Mombasa (now in Kenya) before reaching India and taking up residence in Cochin (now Kochi). Determined to make Portugal the paramount power in the East and to monopolize the spice trade, he erected a series of fortified posts. Under his forceful administration a commercial treaty was concluded with Malacca (now Melaka, Malaysia) and further explorations were undertaken, especially by his son Lourenço. When the Arabs and their Egyptian allies challenged Portuguese dominance, he burned and pillaged their ports and defeated their combined fleet off Diu, India, in February 1509.

When Afonso de Albuquerque arrived at Cochin to supersede him, Almeida, doubting the legality of his commission, imprisoned him. In November 1509, however, he was forced to recognize Albuquerque's authority and set sail for Portugal the next month. While taking on water at Table Bay, Almeida was killed in a skirmish with the local Khoekhoe.

OBADIAH OF BERTINORO

(b. c. 1450, Bertinoro, Papal States—
d. before 1516)

Obadiah (ben Abraham Yare) of Bert was an Italian rabbinic scholar and author. His commentary on the Mishnah (the codification of Jewish Oral Law), incorporating literal explanations from the medieval commentator Rashi and citing rulings from the philosopher

Moses Maimonides, is a standard work of Jewish literature and since its first printing in 1548 has been published in almost every edition of the Mishnah.

Bertinoro is also remembered as the author of three celebrated letters describing his three-year journey (1486–88) to Jerusalem and containing invaluable descriptions of the people and customs of the Jewish communities he visited on the way, from Italy to Palestine. The letters, written to Bertinoro's father and brother during the period 1488–90, have been published under the titles *Darkhei Ẓiyyon* and *HaMassa le-Erez Yisrael* and translated into several languages. He lived in Jerusalem almost continuously after 1488, acting as spiritual head of the Jewish community there.

JOHN CABOT

(b. c. 1450, Genoa? [Italy]—d. c. 1499)

John Cabot (Italian: Giovanni Caboto) was an Italian-born navigator and explorer who, with the sponsorship of King Henry VII of England, voyaged to the northeastern coast of North America in 1497 and 1498. Those journeys helped lay the groundwork for the later British claim to Canada.

The exact details of Cabot's life and of his voyages have remained subjects of debate and controversy among historians and cartographers. He was born in Genoa but moved to Venice in 1461, or possibly earlier, and became a citizen of that city in 1476. While employed by a Venetian mercantile firm, he traveled to the eastern shores of the

John Cabot. Leemage/Universal Images Group/Getty Images

Mediterranean and visited Mecca, a great trading centre where Eastern and Western goods were exchanged. He became skilled in navigational techniques and seems to have envisaged, independently of Christopher Columbus, the possibility of reaching Asia by sailing westward and thus circumventing the long and expensive journeys, replete with many middlemen, of the eastern overland routes.

Cabot's whereabouts and activities from the mid-1480s to the mid-1490s are in doubt, but it is believed that he moved with his family to England and had taken up residence in Bristol by the end of 1495. It is possible that he recognized that a more northerly route westward would be shorter than the lower-latitude route that Columbus had taken in the early 1490s. In early 1496 Henry VII was visiting western England, and on March 5 he issued letters patent to Cabot and his sons, authorizing them to voyage in search of unknown lands, to return their merchandise by the port of Bristol, and to enjoy a monopoly of any trade they might establish there. The news of Columbus' recent discoveries on behalf of Spain was a spur to English action and secured some support for Cabot from Bristol merchants.

In 1496 Cabot made a voyage from Bristol with one ship, but he was forced to turn back because of a shortage of food, inclement weather, and disputes with his crew. In May 1497, however, he set sail from Bristol in the small ship *Matthew*, with a crew of 18 men. He proceeded around Ireland and then north and west, making landfall on the morning of June 24. The exact landing place has never been definitely established, although it was most likely in Canada: it has been variously believed to be in southern Labrador, Newfoundland, or Cape Breton Island. On going ashore, he noticed signs indicating that the area was inhabited but saw no people. Taking posses-sion of the land for the English king, he unfurled both the English and Venetian flags. He conducted explorations from the ship along the coastline, naming various features Cape Discovery, Island of St. John, St. George's Cape, the Trinity Islands, and England's Cape. These may be, respec-tively, the present Cape North, St. Paul Island, Cape Ray, St. Pierre and Miquelon, and Cape Race, all in the area of Cabot Strait.

In the mistaken belief that he had reached the north-east coast of Asia, Cabot returned to Bristol on August 6, 1497. He reported that the land was excellent, the climate temperate, and the sea covered with enough fish to end England's dependence on Iceland's fish. In the midst of an enthusiastic welcome, he announced his plans to return to his landing place and from there sail westward until he came to Japan, the reputed source of spices and gems. Several days later, Henry VII gave him a gift of £10 and granted him an annual pension of £20.

On February 3, 1498, Cabot received new letters pat-ent from the king for a second expedition. His second expedition probably consisted of five ships and about 200 men. Soon after setting out in 1498, one ship was damaged and sought anchorage in Ireland, suggesting that the fleet had been hit by a severe storm. After that the record is scanty and contradictory. In any event, by 1499 it appears that the expedition had been lost at sea and that Cabot had been given up for dead.

The effect of Cabot's efforts was to demonstrate the viability of a short route across the North Atlantic. This would later prove important in the establishment of British colonies in North America.

DIOGO CÃO

(fl. 1480–86)

D iogo Cão (or Cam) was a Portuguese navigator and explorer in the 1480s. He was the first European to discover the mouth of the Congo River (August 1482) and to venture south to the southwestern coast of Africa.

In 1474, King Afonso V entrusted his son, Prince John (later King John II), with the supervision of Portugal's trade with Guinea and the exploration of the western coast of Africa. John sought to close the area to foreign shipping and after his accession in 1481 ordered new voyages of discovery to ascertain the southern limit of the African continent. The navigators were given stone pillars (padrões) to stake the claims of the Portuguese crown. One of the earliest of these expeditions was captained by Diogo Cão, who reached the mouth of the Congo and set up one of the pillars. Sailing a short way upstream, he found that the inhabitants along the banks appeared willing to trade. He then traveled southward along the present Angola coast and erected a second pillar at Cape Santa Maria (Monte Negro, latitude 13°26' S).

Upon his return to Lisbon in 1484, Cão was ennobled by John II, granted an annuity, and authorized to add two pillars to his coat of arms in memory of those he had erected. On a second voyage (1485–86) Cão left a marker at latitude 15°40' S and another after reaching Cape Cross, 21°50' S (now in Namibia); he continued to 22°10' S. Royal hopes that he would reach the Indian Ocean were disappointed, and nothing more is heard of Cão.

BARTOLOMEU DIAS

(b. c. 1450—d. May 29, 1500, at sea, near Cape of Good Hope)

The Portuguese navigator and explorer Bartolomeu Dias (or Diaz) led the first European expedition to round the Cape of Good Hope (1488), and he thus proved the existence of a clear sea route to Asia via the Atlantic and Indian oceans. He was the last—and usually is considered to have been the greatest—of the succession of Portuguese pioneers who progressively explored the Atlantic southward along the coast of Africa during the 15th century.

Virtually nothing is known of Dias' early life. His supposed descent from one of Prince Henry the Navigator's pilots is unproved, and his rank was the comparatively modest one of squire of the royal household. The name "Dias de Novais," once ascribed to him, does not appear to have any foundation.

The Portuguese voyages of discovery had been initiated by Prince Henry and were continued successively by his brother, King Afonso V, and Afonso's son, King John II. At the start of his reign (1481) John ordered new expeditions that were charged with finding the southern limit of Africa. Among the first explorations to be commissioned were undertaken by Diogo Cão, who, on his first voyage (1482–84), reached the mouth of the Congo River and the coast of present-day Angola and, on his second (1485–86), ventured as far south as the coast of present-day Namibia.

On the king's orders Cão had set up stone pillars (padrões) to mark Portuguese overlordship of the areas he visited.

As Cão had not reached the Indian Ocean, John II entrusted command of a new expedition to Dias. In 1486 rumour arose of a great ruler, the Ogané, far to the east, who was identified with the legendary Christian ruler Prester John. John II then sent Pêro da Covilhã and one Afonso Paiva overland to locate India and Abyssinia and ordered Dias to find the southern limit of Africa.

Dias' fleet consisted of three ships, his own São Cristóvão, the São Pantaleão under his associate João Infante, and a supply ship under Dias' brother, whose name is variously given as Pêro or Diogo. The company included some of the leading pilots of the day, among them Pêro de Alenquer and João de Santiago, who earlier had sailed with Cão. In addition, he brought along two black Africans who had been brought back to Portugal by Cão. A 16th-century historian, João de Barros, places Dias' departure in August 1486 and says that he was away 16 months and 17 days, but since two other contemporaries, Duarte Pacheco Pereira and Christopher Columbus, put his return in December 1488, it is now usually supposed that he left in August 1487.

Dias passed Cão's marker, reaching the "Land of St. Barbara" on December 4, Walvis Bay on December 8, and the Gulf of St. Stephen (Elizabeth Bay) on December 26. After January 6, 1488, he was prevented by storms from proceeding along the coast and sailed south out of sight of land for several days. When he again turned to port, no land appeared, and it was only on sailing north that he sighted land on February 3. He had thus rounded the Cape without having seen it. He called the spot Angra de São Brás (Bay of St. Blaise, whose feast day it was) or the Bay of Cowherds, from the people he found there. Dias' black companions were unable to understand these people, who fled but later returned to attack the Portuguese.

The expedition went on to Angra da Roca (present-day Algoa Bay). The crew was unwilling to continue, and Dias recorded the opinions of all his officers, who were unanimously in favour of returning. They agreed to go on for a few days, reaching Rio do Infante, named for the pilot of São Pantaleão; this is almost certainly the present Great Fish (Groot-Vis) River.

Having determined that he had reached the southern tip of Africa and facing strong adverse currents, Dias turned back. He sighted the Cape itself in May. Barros says that Dias named it Cape of Storms and that John II renamed it Cape of Good Hope. Pacheco Pereira, however, attributes the present name to Dias himself, and this is likely since Pacheco Pereira joined Dias at the island of Príncipe. Little is known of the return journey, except that Dias touched at Príncipe, the Rio do Resgate (in the present Liberia), and the fortified trading post of Mina. One of Dias' markers, at Padrão de São Gregório, was retrieved from False Island, about 30 miles (50 km) short of the Great Fish River, in 1938. Another marker once stood at the western end of the Gulf of St. Christopher, since renamed Dias Point.

Nothing is known of Dias' reception by John II. Although plans are said to have been made for a voyage to India, none is known to have been attempted for nine years, perhaps pending news of Pêro da Covilhã. John's successor, Manuel I, authorized Vasco da Gama's celebrated voyage of 1497–99, as well as that of Pedro Álvares Cabral in 1500 that reached the coast of Brazil before heading back east across the Atlantic toward India. Dias, a member of the Cabral expedition, died that May after his ship was lost at sea near the Cape of Good Hope.

Dias had a son, António, and his grandson, Paulo Dias de Novais, governed Angola and became the founder of the first European city in southern Africa, São Paulo de Luanda (now Luanda, Angola), in 1576.

CHRISTOPHER COLUMBUS

(b. between August 26 and October 31?, 1451, Genoa [Italy]—d. May 20, 1506, Valladolid, Spain)

The four transatlantic voyages (1492–93, 1493–96, 1498–1500, and 1502–04) of Italian master navigator and admiral Christopher Columbus (Italian Cristoforo Colombo, Spanish Cristóbal Colón) were the first steps in the process that opened the way for European exploration, exploitation, and colonization of the Americas. He has long been attributed with having "discovered" the New World, but there is now ample evidence that other Europeans—such as Norseman Leif Eriksson—had made it to the shores of North America some five centuries before Columbus embarked on his celebrated first transatlantic expedition. An Italian by birth, Columbus made his voyages under the sponsorship of the Spanish monarchs Ferdinand II and Isabella I of Aragon, Castile, and Leon. He began his quest full of hope and ambition—undoubtedly buoyed by the title "Admiral of the Ocean Sea" that was bestowed upon him by his patrons shortly before his departure in 1492 and by the grants inscribed in the Book of Privileges (a record of his titles and claims)—but he died disappointed and disillusioned.

The period between the quatercentenary (400th anniversary) celebrations of Columbus' achievements in 1892–93 and the quincentenary (500th anniversary) ones of 1992 saw great advances in Columbus scholarship.

Christopher Columbus kneeling before Queen Isabella I. Isabella and her husband, Ferdinand II, sponsored Columbus' voyages and helped establish an overseas Spanish empire. Library of Congress Prints and Photographs Division

Numerous books about Columbus appeared in the 1990s, and the insights of archaeologists and anthropologists began to complement those of sailors and historians. This effort has given rise, as might be expected, to considerable debate. There was also a major shift in approach and interpretation; the older pro-European understanding

29

has given way to one shaped from the perspective of the inhabitants of the Americas themselves. According to the older understanding, the "discovery" of the Americas was a great triumph, one in which Columbus played the part of hero in accomplishing the four voyages, in being the means of bringing great material profit to Spain and to other European countries, and in opening up the Americas to European settlement. The more recent perspective, however, has concentrated on the destructive side of the European conquest, emphasizing, for example, the disastrous impact of the slave trade and the ravages of imported disease on the indigenous peoples of the Caribbean region and the American continents. The sense of triumph has diminished accordingly, and the view of Columbus as hero has now been replaced, for many, by one of a man deeply flawed. While this second perception rarely doubts Columbus' sincerity or abilities as a navigator, it emphatically removes him from his position of honour. Political activists of all kinds have intervened in the debate, further hindering the reconciliation of these disparate views.

EARLY LIFE AND CAREER BEFORE THE FIRST VOYAGE

Little is known of Columbus' early life. The vast majority of scholars, citing Columbus' testament of 1498 and archival documents from Genoa and Savona, believe that he was born in Genoa to a Christian household; however, it has been claimed that he was a converted Jew or that he was born in Spain, Portugal, or elsewhere. Columbus was the eldest son of Domenico Colombo, a Genoese wool worker and merchant, and Susanna Fontanarossa, his wife. His career as a seaman began effectively in the Portuguese merchant marine. After surviving a shipwreck off Cape

St. Vincent at the southwestern point of Portugal in 1476, he based himself in Lisbon, together with his brother Bartholomew. Both were employed as chart makers, but Columbus was principally a seagoing entrepreneur. In 1477 he sailed to Iceland and Ireland with the merchant marine, and in 1478 he was buying sugar in Madeira as an agent for the Genoese firm of Centurioni. In 1479 he met and married Felipa Perestrello e Moniz, a member of an impoverished noble Portuguese family. Their son, Diego, was born in 1480. Between 1482 and 1485 Columbus traded along the Guinea and Gold coasts of tropical West Africa and made at least one voyage to the Portuguese fortress of São Jorge da Mina there, gaining knowledge of Portuguese navigation and the Atlantic wind systems along the way. Felipa died in 1485, and Columbus took as his mistress Beatriz Enríquez de Harana of Córdoba, by whom he had his second son, Ferdinand.

In 1484 Columbus began seeking support for an Atlantic crossing from King John II of Portugal but was denied aid. (Some conspiracy theorists have alleged that Columbus made a secret pact with the monarch, but there is no evidence of this.) By 1486 Columbus was firmly in Spain, asking for patronage from King Ferdinand and Queen Isabella. After at least two rejections, he at last obtained royal support in January 1492. This was achieved chiefly through the interventions of the Spanish treasurer, Luis de Santángel, and of the Franciscan friars of La Rábida, near Huelva, with whom Columbus had stayed in the summer of 1491. Juan Pérez of La Rábida had been one of the queen's confessors and perhaps procured him the crucial audience.

A number of factors—Christian missionary and anti-Islamic fervour, the power of Castile and Aragon, the fear of Portugal, the lust for gold, the desire for adventure, the hope of conquests, and Europe's genuine need for a reliable supply of herbs and spices for cooking, preserving, and medicine—all combined to produce an explosion of energy that launched the first voyage. Columbus had been present at the siege of Granada, which was the last Moorish stronghold to fall to Spain (January 2, 1492), and he was in fact riding back from Granada to La Rábida when he was recalled to the Spanish court and the vital royal audience. Granada's fall had produced euphoria among Spanish Christians and encouraged designs of ultimate triumph over the Islamic world, albeit chiefly, perhaps, by the back way round the globe. A direct assault eastward could prove difficult because the Ottoman Empire and other Islamic states in the region had been gaining strength at a pace that was threatening the Christian monarchies themselves. The Islamic powers had effectively closed the land routes to the East and made the sea route south from the Red Sea extremely hard to access.

In the letter that prefaces his journal of the first voyage, the admiral vividly evokes his own hopes and binds them all together with the conquest of the infidel, the victory of Christianity, and the westward route to discovery and Christian alliance:

> *...and I saw the Moorish king come out of the gates of the city and kiss the royal hands of Your Highnesses... and Your Highnesses, as Catholic Christians...took thought to send me, Christopher Columbus, to the said parts of India, to see those princes and peoples and lands...and the manner which should be used to bring about their conversion to our holy faith, and ordained that I should not go by land to the eastward, by which way it was the custom to go, but by way of the west, by which down to this day we do not know certainly that anyone has passed; therefore, having*

driven out all the Jews from your realms and lord-
ships in the same month of January, Your Highnesses
commanded me that, with a sufficient fleet, I should
go to the said parts of India, and for this accorded
me great rewards and ennobled me so that from that
time henceforth I might style myself "Don" and be
high admiral of the Ocean Sea and viceroy and per-
petual Governor of the islands and continent which
I should discover...and that my eldest son should suc-
ceed to the same position, and so on from generation
to generation forever.

Thus a great number of interests were involved in this adventure, which was, in essence, the attempt to find a route to the rich land of Cathay (China), to India, and to the fabled gold and spice islands of the East by sailing westward over what was presumed to be open sea. Columbus himself clearly hoped to rise from his humble beginnings in this way, to accumulate riches for his family, and to join the ranks of the nobility of Spain. In a similar manner, but at a more exalted level, the Catholic Monarchs hoped that such an enterprise would gain them greater status among the monarchies of Europe, especially against their main rival, Portugal. Then, in alliance with the papacy (in this case, with the Borgia pope Alexander VI [1492–1503]), they might hope to take the lead in the Christian war against the infidel.

At a more elevated level still, Franciscan brethren were preparing for the eventual end of the world, as they believed was prophesied in the Revelation to John. According to that eschatological vision, Christendom would recapture Jerusalem and install a Christian emperor in the Holy Land as a precondition for the coming and defeat of Antichrist, the Christian conversion of the whole human race, and the Last Judgment. Franciscans and others hoped that Columbus' westward project would help to finance a Crusade to the Holy Land that might even be reinforced by, or coordinated with, offensives from the legendary ruler Prester John, who was thought to survive with his descendants in the lands to the east of the infidel. The emperor of Cathay—whom Europeans referred to as the Great Khan of the Golden Horde—was himself held to be interested in Christianity, and Columbus carefully carried a letter of friendship addressed to him by the Spanish monarchs. Finally, the Portuguese explorer Bartolomeu Dias was known to have pressed southward along the coast of West Africa, beyond São Jorge da Mina, in an effort to find an easterly route to Cathay and India by sea. It would never do to allow the Portuguese to find the sea route first.

THE FIRST VOYAGE

The ships for the first voyage—the *Niña*, *Pinta*, and *Santa María*—were fitted out at Palos, on the Tinto River in Spain. Consortia put together by a royal treasury official and composed mainly of Genoese and Florentine bankers in Sevilla (Seville) provided at least 1,140,000 maravedis to outfit the expedition, and Columbus supplied more than a third of the sum contributed by the king and queen. Queen Isabella did not, then, have to pawn her jewels (a myth first put about by Bartolomé de Las Casas in the 16th century).

The little fleet left on August 3, 1492. The admiral's navigational genius showed itself immediately, for they sailed southward to the Canary Islands, off the northwest African mainland, rather than sailing due west to the islands of the Azores. The westerlies prevailing in the Azores had defeated previous attempts to sail to the

Illustration of the three ships—the Niña, *the* Pinta, *and the* Santa María—*that Columbus took on his first voyage.* MPI/Archive Photos/Getty Images

west, but in the Canaries the three ships could pick up the northeast trade winds; supposedly, they could trust to the westerlies for their return. After nearly a month in the Canaries the ships set out from San Sebastián de la Gomera on September 6.

On several occasions in September and early October, sailors spotted floating vegetation and various types of birds—all taken as signs that land was nearby. But by October 10 the crew had begun to lose patience, complaining that with their failure to make landfall, contrary winds and a shortage of provisions would keep them from returning home. Columbus allayed their fears, at least temporarily, and on October 12 land was sighted from the *Pinta* (though Columbus, on the *Niña*, later claimed the privilege for himself). The place of the first Caribbean landfall, called Guanahani, is hotly disputed, but San Salvador (Watlings) Island in the Bahamas is generally preferred to other Bahamian islands (Samana Cay, Rum Cay, or the Plana Cays) or to the Turks and Caicos Islands. Beyond planting the royal banner, however, Columbus spent little time there, being anxious to press on to Cipango, or Cipangu (Japan). He thought that he had found it in Cuba, where he landed on October 28, but he convinced himself by November 1 that Cuba was the Cathay mainland itself, though he had yet to see evidence of great cities. Thus, on December 5, he turned back southeastward to search for the fabled city of Zaiton (Quanzhou, China), missing through this decision his sole chance of setting foot on Florida soil.

Adverse winds carried the fleet to an island called Ayti (Haiti) by its Taino inhabitants; on December 6 Columbus renamed it La Isla Española, or Hispaniola. He seems to have thought that Hispaniola might be Cipango or, if not Cipango, then perhaps one of the legendarily rich isles from which King Solomon's triennial fleet brought back gold, gems, and spices to Jerusalem (1 Kings 10:11, 22); alternatively, he reasoned that the island could be related to the biblical kingdom of Sheba (Saba'). There Columbus found at least enough gold and prosperity to save him from ridicule on his return to Spain. With the help of a Taino cacique, or Indian chief, named Guacanagarí, he set up a stockade on the northern coast of the island, named it La Navidad, and posted 39 men to guard it until his return. The accidental running aground of the *Santa María* provided additional planks and provisions for the garrison.

On January 16, 1493, Columbus left with his remaining two ships for Spain. The journey back was a nightmare. The westerlies did indeed direct them homeward, but in mid-February a terrible storm engulfed the fleet. The *Niña* was driven to seek harbour at Santa Maria in the Azores, where Columbus led a pilgrimage of thanksgiving to the shrine of the Virgin; however, hostile Portuguese authorities temporarily imprisoned the group. After securing their freedom Columbus sailed on, stormbound, and the damaged ship limped to port in Lisbon. There he was obliged to interview with King John II. These events left Columbus under the suspicion of collaborating with Spain's enemies and cast a shadow on his return to Palos on March 15.

On this first voyage many tensions built up that were to remain through all of Columbus' succeeding efforts. First and perhaps most damaging of all, the admiral's apparently high religious and even mystical aspirations were incompatible with the realities of trading, competition, and colonization. Columbus never openly acknowledged this gulf and so was quite incapable of bridging it. The admiral also adopted a mode of sanctification and autocratic leadership that made him many enemies. Moreover, Columbus was determined to take back both material and human cargo to his sovereigns and for himself, and this could be accomplished only if his sailors carried on looting, kidnapping, and other violent acts, especially on Hispaniola. Although he did control some of his men's excesses, these developments blunted his ability to retain the high moral ground and the claim in particular that his "discoveries" were divinely ordained. Further, the Spanish court revived its latent doubts about the foreigner Columbus' loyalty to Spain, and some of Columbus' companions set themselves against him. Captain Pinzón had disputed the route as the fleet reached the Bahamas; he had later sailed the *Pinta* away from Cuba, and Columbus, on November 21, failing to rejoin him until January 6. The *Pinta* made port at Bayona on its homeward journey, separately from Columbus and the *Niña*. Had Pinzón not died so soon after his return, Columbus' command of the second voyage might have been less than assured. As it was, the Pinzón family became his rivals for reward.

THE SECOND AND THIRD VOYAGES

The gold, parrots, spices, and human captives Columbus displayed for his sovereigns at Barcelona convinced all of the need for a rapid second voyage. Columbus was now at the height of his popularity, and he led at least 17 ships out from Cádiz on September 25, 1493. Colonization and Christian evangelization were openly included this time in the plans, and a group of friars shipped with him. The presence of some 1,300 salaried men with perhaps 200 private investors and a small troop of cavalry are testimony to the anticipations for the expedition.

Sailing again via Gomera in the Canary Islands, the fleet took a more southerly course than on the first voyage and reached Dominica in the Lesser Antilles on November

3. After sighting the Virgin Islands, it entered Samaná Bay in Hispaniola on November 23. Michele de Cuneo, deeply impressed by this unerring return, remarked that "since Genoa was Genoa there was never born a man so well equipped and expert in navigation as the said lord Admiral."

An expedition to Navidad four days later was shocked to find the stockade destroyed and the men dead. Here was a clear sign that Taino resistance had gathered strength. More fortified places were rapidly built, including a city, founded on January 2 and named La Isabela for the queen. On February 2 Antonio de Torres left La Isabela with 12 ships, some gold, spices, parrots, and captives (most of whom died en route), as well as the bad news about Navidad and some complaints about Columbus' methods of government. While Torres headed for Spain, two of Columbus' subordinates, Alonso de Ojeda and Pedro Margarit, took revenge for the massacre at Navidad and captured slaves. In March Columbus explored the Cibao Valley (thought to be the gold-bearing region of the island) and established the fortress of St. Thomas (Santo Tomás) there. Then, late in April, Columbus led the *Niña* and two other ships to explore the Cuban coastline and search for gold in Jamaica, only to conclude that Hispaniola promised the richest spoils for the settlers. The admiral decided that Hispaniola was indeed the biblical land of Sheba and that Cuba was the mainland of Cathay. On June 12, 1494, Columbus insisted that his men swear a declaration to that effect—an indication that he intended to convince his sovereign he had reached Cathay, though not all of Columbus' company agreed with him. The following year he began a determined conquest of Hispaniola, spreading devastation among the Taino. There is evidence, especially in the objections of a friar, Bernardo Buil, that Columbus' methods remained harsh.

The admiral departed La Isabela for Spain on March 10, 1496, leaving his brothers, Bartholomew and Diego, in charge of the settlement. He reached Cádiz on June 11 and immediately pressed his plans for a third voyage upon his sovereigns, who were at Burgos. Spain was then at war with France and needed to buy and keep its alliances; moreover, the yield from the second voyage had fallen well short of the investment. Portugal was still a threat, though the two nations had divided the Atlantic conveniently between themselves in the Treaty of Tordesillas (June 7, 1494). According to the treaty, Spain might take all land west of a line drawn from pole to pole 370 leagues— i.e., about 1,185 miles (1,910 km)—west of the Cape Verde Islands, whereas Portugal could claim land to the east of the line. But what about the other side of the world, where West met East? Also, there might be a previously undiscovered antipodean continent. Who, then, should be trusted to draw the line there? Ferdinand and Isabella therefore made a cautious third investment. Six ships left Sanlúcar de Barrameda on May 30, 1498, three filled with explorers and three with provisions for the settlement on Hispaniola. It was clear now that Columbus was expected both to find great prizes and to establish the flag of Spain firmly in the East.

Certainly he found prizes, but not quite of the kind his sponsors required. His aim was to explore to the south of the existing discoveries, in the hope of finding both a strait from Cuba (his "Cathay") to India and, perhaps, the unknown antipodean continent. On June 21 the provision ships left Gomera for Hispaniola, while the explorers headed south for the Cape Verde Islands. Columbus began the Atlantic crossing on July 4 from São Tiago Island in Cape Verde. He discovered the principle of compass variation (the variation at any point on Earth's surface between the direction to magnetic and geographic north), for which he made brilliant allowance on the journey from Margarita Island to Hispaniola on the later leg of this voyage, and he also observed, though misunderstood, the diurnal rotation of the northern polestar (Polaris). After stopping at Trinidad (named for the Holy Trinity, whose protection he had invoked for the voyage), Columbus entered the Gulf of Paria and planted the Spanish flag on the Paria Peninsula in Venezuela. He sent the caravel *El Corréo* southward to investigate the mouth of the Grande River (a northern branch of the Orinoco River delta), and by August 15 he knew by the great torrents of fresh water flowing into the Gulf of Paria that he had discovered another continent—"another world." But he did not find the strait to India, nor did he find King Solomon's gold mines, which his reading had led him and his sovereigns to expect in these latitudes; and he made only disastrous discoveries when he returned to Hispaniola.

Both the Taino and the European immigrants had resented the rule of Bartholomew and Diego Columbus. A rebellion by the mayor of La Isabela, Francisco Roldán, had led to appeals to the Spanish court, and, even as Columbus attempted to restore order (partly by hangings), the Spanish chief justice, Francisco de Bobadilla, was on his way to the colony with a royal commission to investigate the complaints. It is hard to explain exactly what the trouble was. Columbus' report to his sovereigns from the second voyage, taken back by Torres and so known as the Torres Memorandum, speaks of sickness, poor provisioning, recalcitrant natives, and undisciplined hidalgos (gentry). It may be that these problems had intensified. But the Columbus family must be held at least partly responsible, intent as it was on enslaving the Taino and shipping them to Europe or forcing them to mine gold on Hispaniola. Under Columbus' original system of gold production, local chiefs had been in charge of

Columbus, in chains after being placed under arrest by Bobadilla, walks among onlookers and admirers. Hulton Archive/Getty Images

delivering gold on a loose per capita basis; the adelantado (governor) Bartholomew Columbus had replaced that policy with a system of direct exploitation led by favoured Spaniards, causing widespread dissent among unfavoured Spaniards and indigenous chiefs. Bobadilla ruled against the Columbus family when he arrived in Hispaniola. He clapped Columbus and his two brothers in irons and sent them promptly back on the ship *La Gorda*, and they arrived at Cádiz in late October 1500.

During that return journey Columbus composed a long letter to his sovereigns that is one of the most extraordinary he wrote, and one of the most informative. One part of its exalted, almost mystical, quality may be attributed to the humiliations the admiral had endured (humiliations he compounded by refusing to allow the captain of the *La Gorda* to remove his chains during the voyage) and another to the fact that he was now suffering severely from sleeplessness, eyestrain, and a form of rheumatoid arthritis, which may have hastened his death. Much of what he said in the letter, however, seems genuinely to have expressed his beliefs. It shows that Columbus had absolute faith in his navigational abilities, his seaman's sense of the weather, his eyes, and his reading. He asserted that he had reached the outer region of the Earthly Paradise, in that, during his earlier approach to Trinidad and the Paria Peninsula, the polestar's rotation had given him the impression that the fleet was climbing. The weather had become extremely mild, and the flow of fresh water into the Gulf of Paria was, as he saw, enormous. All this could have one explanation only—they had mounted toward the temperate heights of the Earthly Paradise, heights from which the rivers of Paradise ran into the sea. Columbus had found all such signs of the outer regions of the Earthly Paradise in his reading, and indeed they were widely known. On this estimate, he was therefore close to the realms of gold that lay near Paradise. He had not found the gold yet, to be sure, but he knew where it was. Columbus' expectations thus allowed him to interpret his discoveries in terms of biblical and Classical sources and to do so in a manner that would be comprehensible to his sponsors and favourable to himself.

This letter, desperate though it was, convinced the sovereigns that, even if he had not yet found the prize, he had been close to it after all. They ordered his release and gave him audience at Granada in late December 1500. They accepted that Columbus' capacities as navigator and explorer were unexcelled, although he was an unsatisfactory governor, and on Sept. 3, 1501, they appointed Nicolás de Ovando to succeed Bobadilla to the governorship. Columbus, though ill and importunate, was a better investment than the many adventurers and profiteers who had meantime been licensed to compete with him, and there was always the danger (revealed in some of the letters of this period) that he would offer his services to his native Genoa. In October 1501 Columbus went to Sevilla to make ready his fourth and final expedition.

THE FOURTH VOYAGE AND FINAL YEARS

The winter and spring of 1501–02 were exceedingly busy. The four chosen ships were bought, fitted, and crewed, and some 20 of Columbus' extant letters and memoranda were written then, many in exculpation of Bobadilla's charges, others pressing even harder the nearness of the Earthly Paradise and the need to reconquer Jerusalem. Columbus took to calling himself "Christbearer" in his letters and to using a strange and mystical signature, never satisfactorily explained. He began also, with all these thoughts and pressures in mind, to compile his *Book of Privileges*, which defends the titles and financial claims of the Columbus family, and his apocalyptic *Book of Prophecies*, which includes several biblical passages. The first compilation seems an odd companion to the second, yet both were closely linked in the admiral's own mind. He seems to have been certain that his mission was divinely guided. Thus, the loftiness of his spiritual aspirations increased as the threats to his personal ones mounted. In the midst of all these efforts and hazards, Columbus sailed from Cádiz on his fourth voyage on May 9, 1502.

Columbus' sovereigns had lost much of their confidence in him, and there is much to suggest that pity mingled with hope in their support. His four ships contrasted sharply with the 30 granted to the governor Ovando. His illnesses were worsening, and the hostility to his rule in Hispaniola was unabated. Thus, Ferdinand and Isabella forbade him to return there. He was to resume, instead, his interrupted exploration of the "other world" to the south that he had found on his third voyage and to look particularly for gold and the strait to India. Columbus expected to meet the Portuguese navigator Vasco da Gama in the East, and the sovereigns instructed him on the appropriate courteous behaviour for such a meeting— another sign, perhaps, that they did not wholly trust him. They were right. He departed from Gran Canaria on the night of May 25, made landfall at Martinique on June 15 (after the fastest crossing to date), and was, by June 29, demanding entrance to Santo Domingo on Hispaniola. Only on being refused entry by Ovando did he sail away to the west and south. From July to September 1502 he explored the coast of Jamaica, the southern shore of Cuba, Honduras, and the Mosquito Coast of Nicaragua. His feat of Caribbean transnavigation, which took him to Bonacca Island off Cape Honduras on July 30, deserves to be reckoned on a par, as to difficulty, with that of crossing the Atlantic, and the admiral was justly proud of it. The fleet continued southward along Costa Rica. Constantly probing for the strait, Columbus sailed around the Chiriquí Lagoon (in Panama) in October; then, searching for gold, he explored the Panamanian region of Veragua (Veraguas) in the foulest of weather. In order to exploit the promising gold yield he was beginning to find there, the admiral in February 1503 attempted to establish a trading post at Santa María de Belén on the bank of the Belén (Bethlehem) River under the command of Bartholomew Columbus. However, Indian resistance and the poor condition of his ships (of which only two remained, fearfully holed by shipworm) caused him to turn back to Hispaniola. On this voyage disaster again struck. Against Columbus' better judgment, his pilots turned the fleet north too soon. The ships could not make the distance and had to be beached on the coast of Jamaica. By June 1503 Columbus and his crews were castaways.

Columbus had hoped, as he said to his sovereigns, that "my hard and troublesome voyage may yet turn out to be my noblest"; it was in fact the most disappointing of all and the most unlucky. In its explorations the fleet had missed discovering the Pacific (across the isthmus of Panama) and failed to make contact with the Maya of Yucatán by the narrowest of margins. Two of the men—Diego Méndez and Bartolomeo Fieschi, captains of the wrecked ships *La Capitana* and *Vizcaíno*, respectively—left about July 17 by canoe to get help for the castaways; although they managed to traverse the 450 miles (720 km) of open sea to Hispaniola, Ovando made no great haste to deliver that help. In the meantime, the admiral displayed his acumen once again by correctly predicting an eclipse of the Moon from his astronomical tables, thus frightening the local peoples into providing food; but rescuers did not arrive until June 1504, and Columbus and his men did not reach Hispaniola until August 13 of that year. On November 7 he sailed back to Sanlúcar and found that Queen Isabella, his main supporter, had made her will and was dying.

Columbus always maintained that he had found the true Indies and Cathay in the face of mounting evidence that he had not. Perhaps he genuinely believed that he had been there; in any event, his disallowances of the "New World" hindered his goals of nobility and wealth and dented his later reputation. Columbus had been remote from his companions and intending colonists, and he had been a poor judge of the ambitions, and perhaps the failings, of those who sailed with him. This combination proved damaging to almost all of his hopes. Nonetheless, it would be wrong to suppose that Columbus spent his final two years wholly in illness, poverty, and oblivion. His son Diego was well established at court, and the admiral himself lived in Sevilla in some style. His "tenth" of the gold diggings in Hispaniola, guaranteed in 1493, provided a substantial revenue (against which his Genoese bankers allowed him to draw), and one of the few ships to escape a hurricane off Hispaniola in 1502 (in which Bobadilla himself went down) was that carrying Columbus' gold. He felt himself ill-used and shortchanged nonetheless, and these years were marred, for both him and King Ferdinand, by his constant pressing for redress. Columbus followed the court from Segovia to Salamanca and Valladolid, attempting to gain an audience. He knew that his life was nearing its end, and in August 1505 he began to amend his will. He died on May 20, 1506. First he was laid in the Franciscan friary in Valladolid, then taken to the family mausoleum established at the Carthusian monastery of Las Cuevas in Sevilla. In 1542, by the will of his son Diego, Columbus' bones were laid with his own in the Cathedral of Santo

Domingo, Hispaniola (now in the Dominican Republic). After Spain ceded Hispaniola to France, the remains were moved to Havana, Cuba, in 1795 and returned to Sevilla in 1898. In 1877, however, workers at the cathedral in Santo Domingo claimed to have found another set of bones that were marked as those of Columbus. Since 1992 these bones have been interred in the Columbus Lighthouse (Faro a Colón).

PRINCIPAL EVIDENCE OF TRAVELS

There are few material remains of Columbus' travels. Efforts to find the Spaniards' first settlement on Hispaniola have so far failed, but the present-day fishing village of Bord de Mer de Limonade (near Cap-Haïtien, Haiti) may be close to the original site, and a Taino chieftain's settlement has been identified nearby. Concepción de la Vega, which Columbus founded on the second voyage, may be the present La Vega Vieja, in the Dominican Republic. Remains at the site of La Isabela are still to be fully excavated, as are those at Sevilla la Nueva, Jamaica, where Columbus' two caravels were beached on the fourth voyage. The techniques of skeletal paleopathology and paleodemography are being applied with some success to determine the fates of the native populations.

WRITTEN SOURCES

The majority of the surviving primary sources about Columbus are not private diaries or missives; instead, they were intended to be read by other people. There is, then, an element of manipulation about them—a fact that must be borne fully in mind for their proper understanding.

48

Foremost among these sources are the journals written by Columbus himself for his sovereigns—one for the first voyage, now lost though partly reconstructed; one for the second, almost wholly gone; and one for the third, which, like the first, is accessible through reconstructions made by using later quotations. Each of the journals may be supplemented by letters and reports to and from the sovereigns and their trusted officials and friends, provisioning decrees from the sovereigns, and, in the case of the second voyage, letters and reports of letters from fellow voyagers (especially Michele da Cuneo, Diego Alvarez Chanca, and Guillermo Coma). There is no journal and only one letter from the fourth voyage, but a complete roster and payroll survive from this, alone of all the voyages; in addition, an eyewitness account survives that has been plausibly attributed to Columbus' younger son, Ferdinand (born c. 1488), who traveled with the admiral. Further light is thrown upon the explorations by the so-called Pleitos de Colón, judicial documents concerning Columbus' disputed legacy. A more recent discovery is a copybook that purportedly contains five narrative letters and two personal ones from Columbus, all previously unknown, as well as additional copies of two known letters—all claimed as authentic. Supplemental narratives include *The Life of the Admiral Christopher Columbus*, which has been attributed to Ferdinand Columbus, the *Historia de los Reyes Católicos* (c. 1500) of Andrés Bernáldez (a friend of Columbus and chaplain to the archbishop of Sevilla), and the *Historia de las Indias*, which was compiled about 1550–63 by Bartolomé de Las Casas (former bishop of Chiapas and a champion of the indigenous people of the Americas).

Columbus' intentions and presuppositions may be better understood by examining the few books still extant from his own library. Some of these were

extensively annotated, often by the admiral and sometimes by his brother Bartholomew, including copies of
the *Imago mundi* by the 15th-century French theologian
Pierre d'Ailly (a compendium containing a great number of cosmological and theological texts), the *Historia
rerum ubique gestarum* of Pope Pius II, published in 1477,
the version of *The Travels of Marco Polo* known as the
De consuetudinibus et condicionibus orientalium regionum of
Francesco Pipino (1483–85), Alfonso de Palencia's late
15th-century Castilian translation of Plutarch's *Parallel
Lives*, and the humanist Cristoforo Landino's Italian
translation of the *Natural History* of Pliny the Elder.
Other books known to have been in Columbus' possession are the *Guide to Geography* of the ancient astronomer
and geographer Ptolemy, the *Catholicon* of the 15th-
century encyclopaedist John of Genoa, and a popular
handbook to confession, the *Confessionale* produced by
the Dominican St. Antoninus of Florence. The whole
shows that the admiral was adept in Latin, Castilian, and
Italian, if not expert in all three. He annotated primarily
in Latin and Spanish, very rarely in Italian. He had probably already read and annotated at least the first three
named texts before he set out on his first voyage to the
"Indies." Columbus was a deeply religious and reflective
man as well as a distinguished seaman, and, being largely
self-taught, he had a reverence for learning, perhaps
especially the learning of his most influential Spanish
supporters. A striking manifestation of his sensibilities
is the *Book of Prophecies*, a collection of pronouncements
largely taken from the Bible and seeming to bear directly
on his role in the western voyages; the book was probably compiled by Columbus and his friend the Carthusian
friar Gaspar Gorricio between September 1501 and
March 1502, with additions until circa 1505.

CALCULATIONS

Contrary to common lore, Columbus never thought that the world was flat. Educated Europeans had known that Earth was spherical in shape since at least the early 7th century, when the popular *Etymologies* of St. Isidore of Sevilla were produced in Spain. Columbus' miscalculations, such as they were, lay in other areas. First, his estimate of the sea distance to be crossed to Cathay was wildly inaccurate. Columbus rejected Ptolemy's estimate of the journey from West to East overland, substituting a far longer one based on a chart (now lost) supplied by the Florentine mathematician and geographer Paolo Toscanelli, and on Columbus' preference for the calculations of the Classical geographer Marinus of Tyre. Additionally, Columbus' reading primarily of the 13th–14th-century Venetian Marco Polo's *Travels* gave him the idea that the lands of the East stretched out far around the back of the globe, with the island of Cipango—itself surrounded by islands—located a further 1,500 miles (2,400 km) from the mainland of Cathay. He seems to have argued that this archipelago might be near the Azores. Columbus also read the seer Salathiel-Ezra in the books of Esdras, from the *Apocrypha* (especially 2 Esdras 6:42, in which the prophet states that Earth is six parts land to one of water), thus reinforcing these ideas of the proportion of land- to sea-crossing. The mistake was further compounded by his idiosyncratic view of the length of a degree of geographic latitude. The degree, according to Arabic calculators, consisted of 56 ⅔ Arab miles, and an Arab mile measured 6,481 feet (1,975.5 metres). Given that a nautical mile measures 6,076 feet (1,852 metres), this degree amounts to approximately 60.45 nautical miles (112 km). Columbus, however, used the Italian mile of 4,847 feet (1,477.5 metres) for his computations and thus arrived at approximately 45 nautical miles (83 km) to a degree. This shortened the supposed distance across the sea westward to such an extent that Zaiton, Marco Polo's great port of Cathay, would have lain a little to the east of present-day San Diego, California, U.S.; also, the islands of Cipango would have been about as far north of the Equator as the Virgin Islands—close to where Columbus actually made his landfalls.

The miscalculation of distance may have been willful on Columbus' part and made with an eye to his sponsors. The first journal suggests that Columbus may have been aware of his inaccuracy, for he consistently concealed from his sailors the great number of miles they had covered, lest they become fearful for the journey back. Such manipulations may be interpreted as evidence of bravery and the need to inspire confidence rather than of simple dishonesty or error.

ASSESSMENT

The debate about Columbus' character and achievements began at least as early as the first rebellion of the Taino Indians and continued with Roldán, Bobadilla, and Ovando. It has been revived periodically (notably by Las Casas and Jean-Jacques Rousseau) ever since. The Columbus quincentenary of 1992 rekindled the intensity of this early questioning and redirected its aims, often with insightful results. The word "encounter" is now preferred to "discovery" when describing the contacts between Europe and the Americas, and more attention has been paid to the fate of indigenous Americans and to the perspectives of non-Christians. Enlightening discoveries have been made about the diseases that reached the New World through Columbus' agency as well as those his sailors took back with them to the Old. The pendulum may, however, have swung too far. Columbus has been blamed for events far beyond his own reach or knowledge, and too little attention has been paid to the historical circumstances that conditioned him. His obsessions with lineage and imperialism, his zealous religious beliefs, his enslaving of indigenous peoples, and his execution of colonial subjects come from a world remote from that of modern democratic ideas, but it was the world to which he belonged. The forces of European expansion, with their slaving and search for gold, had been unleashed before him and were quite beyond his control; he simply decided to be in their vanguard. He succeeded. Columbus' towering stature as a seaman and navigator, the sheer power of his religious convictions (self-delusory as they sometimes were), his personal magnetism, his courage, his endurance, his determination, and, above all, his achievements as an explorer should continue to be recognized.

AFONSO DE ALBUQUERQUE

(b. 1453, Alhandra, near Lisbon—d. December 15, 1515, at sea, off Goa, India)

Portuguese soldier Afonso de Albuquerque, the Great, was the conqueror of Goa (1510) in India and of Malacca (Melaka; 1511) on the Malay Peninsula. His program to gain control of all the main maritime trade routes of the East and to build permanent fortresses with settled populations laid the foundations of Portuguese hegemony in South and Southeast Asia.

Albuquerque was the second son of the senhor (lord) of Vila Verde. His paternal great-grandfather and grandfather had been confidential secretaries to kings John I and Edward (Duarte); his maternal grandfather had been admiral of Portugal. Albuquerque served 10 years in North Africa, where he gained early military experience crusading against Muslims. He was present at Afonso V's conquest of Arzila and Tangier in 1471. King John II (ruled 1481–95) made him master of the horse, a post Albuquerque held throughout the reign. In 1489 he again served in North Africa at the defense of Graciosa. Under John's successor, Manuel I, Albuquerque was less prominent at court but again served in Morocco.

Although Albuquerque made his mark under the stern John II and gained his experience in Africa, his reputation rests on his service in the East. When Vasco da Gama returned to Portugal in 1499 from his pioneering voyage around the Cape of Good Hope to India, King Manuel straightway sent a second fleet under Pedro Álvares Cabral to open relations and trade with the Indian rulers. The Muslim traders who had monopolized the distribution of spices turned the zamorin, or Hindu prince of Calicut (modern Kozhikode), against the Portuguese. His dependency, Cochin (Kochi), on the southwestern Indian coast, however, welcomed them. In 1503 Albuquerque arrived with his cousin Francisco to protect the ruler of Cochin, where he built the first Portuguese fortress in Asia and placed a garrison. After setting up a trading post at Quilon, he returned to Lisbon in July 1504, where he was well received by Manuel and participated in the formulation of policy. In 1505 Manuel appointed Dom Francisco de Almeida first governor in India, with the rank of viceroy. Almeida's object was to develop trade and aid the allies of the Portuguese. Albuquerque left Lisbon with Tristão da Cunha in April 1506 to explore the east coast of Africa and build a fortress on the island of Socotra to block the mouth of the Red Sea and cut off Arab trade with India. This done (August 1507), Albuquerque captured Hormuz (Ormuz), an island in the channel between the Persian Gulf and the Gulf of Oman, to open Persian trade with Europe. His project of building a fortress at Hormuz had to be abandoned because of differences with his captains, who departed for India. Albuquerque, though left with only two ships, continued to raid the coasts of the Persian and Arabian seas.

King Manuel appointed Albuquerque to succeed Almeida at the end of Almeida's term, though without the rank of viceroy. When Albuquerque reached India in December 1508, Almeida had crushed the improvised sea force of Calicut, but a navy from Egypt had defeated and killed his son. Insisting on retaining power until he had avenged his son's death, Almeida, to avoid interference, had Albuquerque imprisoned. Almeida defeated the Muslims off Diu in February 1509, and it was only in the following November, with the arrival of a fleet from Portugal, that he finally turned his office over to Albuquerque.

Albuquerque's plan was to assume active control over all the main maritime trade routes of the East and to establish permanent fortresses with settled populations. His attempt to seize Cochin in January 1510 was unsuccessful. By February Albuquerque had realized that it was better to try to supplant the Muslims; assisted by a powerful corsair named Timoja, he took 23 ships to attack Goa, long ruled by Muslim princes. He occupied it in March 1510, was forced out of the citadel by a Muslim army in May, and was finally able to carry it by assault in November. The Muslim defenders were all killed.

After this victory over the Muslims, the Hindu rulers accepted the Portuguese presence in India. Albuquerque planned to use Goa as a naval base against the Muslims, to divert the spice trade to it, and to use it to supply Persian horses to the Hindu princes. By marrying his men to the widows of his victims he would give Goa its own population, and its supplies would be assured by the village communities under a special regime. After providing for the government of Goa, Albuquerque embarked on the conquest of Malacca, on the Malay Peninsula, the immediate point of distribution for the Spice Islands and points east. He took that port in July 1511, garrisoned it, and sent ships in search of spices.

In the meantime Goa was again under heavy attack. He left in January 1512 and relieved Goa. Having established himself there and having gained control over the movement of goods by a licensing system, Albuquerque again turned to the Red Sea, taking a force of Portuguese and Indians. Because Socotra was inadequate as a base, he attempted to take Aden, but his forces proved insufficient. He thereupon explored the coasts of Arabia and Abyssinia (modern Ethiopia). Returning to India, he finally subdued Calicut, hitherto the main seat of opposition to the Portuguese.

In February 1515 he again left Goa with 26 ships for Hormuz, gaining control of part of the island. He was taken ill in September and turned back to Goa. On the way he learned that he had been superseded by his personal enemy, Lope Soares; he died embittered on shipboard before reaching his destination.

Albuquerque's plans derived from the crusading spirit of John II and others. He did not allow himself to be diverted from his schemes by considerations of mercantile gain. His boldest concepts, such as turning the Persians against the Turks or ruining Egypt by diverting the course of the Nile, were perhaps superhuman, but so perhaps was his achievement.

AMERIGO VESPUCCI

(b. 1454?, Florence, Italy—d. 1512, Sevilla
[Seville], Spain)

The Italian-born Spanish merchant and explorer-navigator Amerigo Vespucci, a contemporary of

Amerigo Vespucci, portrait by an unknown artist; in the Uffizi Gallery, Florence. Alinari/Art Resource, New York

Christopher Columbus (whom he befriended in 1505), took part in two important early voyages to the New World, in 1499–1500 and 1501–02. Those journeys convinced him and others that the newly discovered lands west of the Atlantic were not part of Asia but constituted a separate landmass. Soon, the term *America*, a derivation of his given name, had become associated with this new land.

Vespucci was the son of a notary named Nastagio. His uncle, Giorgio Antonio, gave the boy a humanistic education. In 1479 Vespucci accompanied another relation, who had been sent by the famous Italian Medici family to be the family spokesman to the king of France. On returning, Vespucci entered the "bank" of Lorenzo and Giovanni di Pierfrancesco de' Medici and gained the confidence of his employers. At the end of 1491 they sent Vespucci to Sevilla (Seville) in Spain, where their agent, Giannotto Berardi, appears to have been engaged partly in fitting out ships. Vespucci was probably present when Columbus returned in 1493 from his first expedition, which Berardi had assisted. Later Vespucci was to collaborate, still with Berardi, in the preparation of a ship for Columbus' second expedition and of others for his third. When Berardi died, either at the end of 1495 or at the beginning of 1496, Vespucci became manager of the Sevilla agency.

THE VOYAGES

The period during which Vespucci made his voyages falls between 1497 and 1504. Two series of documents on his voyages are extant. The first series consists of a letter in the name of Vespucci from Lisbon, Portugal, dated September 4, 1504, written in Italian, perhaps to the *gonfalonier* (magistrate of a medieval Italian republic) Piero Soderini, and printed in Florence in 1505; and of two Latin versions of this letter, printed under the titles of "Quattuor Americi navigationes" and "Mundus Novus," or "Epistola Alberici de Novo Mundo." The second series consists of three private letters addressed to the Medici. In the first series of documents, four voyages by Vespucci are mentioned; in the second, only two. Until the 1930s the documents of the first series were considered from the point of view of the order of the four voyages. According to a theory of Alberto Magnaghi, on the contrary, these documents are to be regarded as the result of skillful manipulations, and the sole authentic papers would be the private letters, so the verified voyages would be reduced to two. The question is fundamental for the evaluation of Vespucci's work and has given rise to fierce controversy; attempts to reconcile the two series of documents cannot generally be considered successful.

The voyage completed by Vespucci between May 1499 and June 1500 as navigator of an expedition of four ships sent from Spain under the command of Alonso de Ojeda is certainly authentic. (This is the second expedition of the traditional series.) Since Vespucci took part as navigator, he certainly cannot have been inexperienced; but it does not seem possible that he had made a previous voyage (1497–98) in this area (i.e., around the Gulf of Mexico and the Atlantic coast from Florida to Chesapeake Bay), though this matter remains unresolved.

In the voyage of 1499–1500 Vespucci would seem to have left Ojeda after reaching the coast of what is now Guyana. Turning south, he is believed to have discovered the mouth of the Amazon River and to have gone as far as Cape St. Augustine (latitude about 6° S). On the way back he reached Trinidad, sighted the mouth of the Orinoco River, and then made for Haiti. Vespucci thought he had sailed along the coast of the extreme easterly peninsula of Asia, where Ptolemy, the geographer, believed the market of Cattigara to be; so he looked for the tip of this peninsula, calling it Cape Cattigara. He supposed that the ships, once past that point, emerged into the seas of southern Asia. As soon as he was back in Spain, he equipped a fresh expedition with the aim of reaching the Indian Ocean, the Gulf of the Ganges (modern Bay of Bengal), and the island of Taprobane or Ceylon (now Sri Lanka). But the Spanish government did not welcome his proposals, and at the end of 1500 Vespucci went into the service of Portugal.

Under Portuguese auspices Vespucci completed a second expedition, which set off from Lisbon on May 13, 1501. After a halt at the Cape Verde Islands, the expedition traveled southwestward and reached the coast of Brazil toward Cape St. Augustine. The remainder of the voyage is disputed, but Vespucci claimed to have continued southward, and he may have sighted (January 1502) Guanabara Bay (at present-day Rio de Janeiro) and sailed as far as the Río de la Plata, making Vespucci the first European to discover that estuary (Juan Díaz de Solís arrived there in 1516). The ships may have journeyed still farther south, along the coast of Patagonia (in present-day southern Argentina). The return route is unknown. Vespucci's ships anchored at Lisbon on July 22, 1502.

VESPUCCI'S NAMESAKE AND REPUTATION

The voyage of 1501–02 is of fundamental importance in the history of geographic discovery in that Vespucci himself, and scholars as well, became convinced that the newly discovered lands were not part of Asia but a "New World." In 1507 a humanist, Martin Waldseemüller, reprinted at Saint-Dié in Lorraine the "Quattuor Americi navigationes" ("Four Voyages of Amerigo"), preceded by a pamphlet

Vespucci at sea. © Pantheon/SuperStock

of his own entitled "Cosmographiae introductio," and he suggested that the newly discovered world be named "ab Americo Inventore...quasi Americi terram sive Americam" ("from Amerigo the discoverer...as if it were the land of Americus or America"). The proposal is perpetuated in a large planisphere of Waldseemüller's, in which the name America appears for the first time, although applied only to South America. The suggestion caught on; the extension of the name to North America, however, came later. On the upper part of the map, with the hemisphere comprising the Old World, appears the picture of Ptolemy; on the part of the map with the New World hemisphere is the picture of Vespucci.

It is uncertain whether Vespucci took part in yet another expedition (1503–04) for the Portuguese government (it is said that he may have been with one under Gonzalo Coelho). In any case, that expedition contributed no fresh knowledge. Although Vespucci subsequently helped to prepare other expeditions, he never again joined one in person.

At the beginning of 1505 he was summoned to the court of Spain for a private consultation and, as a man of experience, was engaged to work for the Casa de Contratación (House of Commerce), popularly called Casa de las Indias (House of the Indies). The firm, which had been founded two years earlier at Sevilla, controlled the royal monopoly of commerce with the New World. In 1508 the house appointed him to the influential post of *piloto mayor* (master navigator), a position of great responsibility, which included the examination of the pilots' and ships' masters' licenses for voyages. He also had to prepare the official map of newly discovered lands and of the routes to them (for the royal survey), interpreting and coordinating all data that the captains were obliged to furnish. Vespucci, who had obtained Spanish citizenship, held this position until his death. His widow, Maria Cerezo, was granted a pension in recognition of her husband's great services.

Some scholars have held Vespucci to be a usurper of the merits of others. Yet, despite the possibly deceptive claims made by him or advanced on his behalf, he was a genuine pioneer of Atlantic exploration and a vivid contributor to the early travel literature of the New World.

PÊRO DA COVILHÃ

(b. c. 1460, Covilhã, Portugal—d. after 1526)

The early Portuguese explorer of western India and eastern Africa Pêro Covilhã (also spelled Pedro de Covilham, or Pedro de Covilhão) is best remembered for helping to establish relations between Portugal and Abyssinia (modern Ethiopia).

The young Pêro served the duke of Medina-Sidonia in Sevilla (Seville) for six or seven years. He returned to Portugal with the duke's brother late in 1474 or early in 1475, at which time he passed into the service of King Afonso V, first as a junior squire and then as squire, serving with horse and arms. Pêro accompanied Afonso when the king claimed the Castilian throne and was proclaimed at Plasencia, and he was present at the Battle of Toro. He also escorted the king on a fruitless journey to France to seek aid from Louis XI. After Afonso's death in 1481, Pêro served his son and successor, John II, as a squire of the royal guard and was employed as a confidential messenger to Spain. He was sent on two missions to North Africa, one, in the guise of a merchant, to seek the friendship of the ruler of Tlemcen (now in Algeria), and the other to Fez (Morocco) to buy horses for Dom Manuel, later king (as Manuel I).

John II hoped to profit from the spice trade of India and to make contact with the Christian ruler of Abyssinia, identified with the semimythical Prester John. Abyssinians had already visited Rome and even the Iberian Peninsula. John had sent Diogo Cão (Diogo Cam) southward along the west coast of Africa, and he had discovered the Congo River and sailed beyond, but Cão's belief that he had reached or was about to reach the cape proved unfounded. John then ordered Bartolomeu Dias to pursue Cão's explorations. He also decided to send travelers by land to report on the location and trade of India and Abyssinia. This move may have resulted from reports received in 1486 in Benin (a kingdom on the west coast of Africa), referring to a great ruler far to the east. Pêro was chosen for the mission to India, and Afonso de Paiva, a squire who spoke Arabic, was to seek Prester John and discover a route from Guinea to Abyssinia.

The men left Portugal in May 1487 with letters of credit on Italian bankers; they reached Barcelona and sailed to Naples and Rhodes, where they assumed the guise of honey merchants and sailed to Alexandria. They became ill, and their wares were seized, but they bought other goods and went to Cairo, joining a group of North Africans traveling to Aden. There they separated, Pêro going to India, reaching Cannanore (now Kannur), Calicut (Kozhikode), and Goa. He then returned to Ormuz (Hormuz), in Persia, sometime between October 1489 and March 1490. Meanwhile, Afonso de Paiva had reached Abyssinia. The two had proposed to meet at Cairo. Pêro arrived there about the end of 1490 or early 1491 and received news of his companion's death. Meanwhile, John II had sent two messengers to Cairo to instruct Pêro to return when the mission was completed.

Pêro wrote a letter to John about his experiences and continued on to Abyssinia. One of the messengers accompanied him to Ormuz, where they separated. Pêro made his way to the Red Sea. Disguised as a Muslim, he visited Mecca and Medina. He also saw Mount Sinai, reaching Zeila in 1492 or 1493, whence he passed by caravan to Abyssinia, where he was destined to spend the rest of his life.

Pêro was received by the Abyssinian ruler, Emperor Eskender, and was well treated and made governor of a district. He was not, however, allowed to leave the country. Some years later the Abyssinian regent, Queen Helena, sent an Armenian named Matthew to Portugal. He reached Afonso de Albuquerque at Goa in 1512 and was in Portugal in 1514. It was then decided to send a Portuguese embassy to Abyssinia. The first ambassador died, and his successor, Dom Rodrigo de Lima, and his party left from India in 1517 and finally reached the emperor's camp in December 1520. They found Pêro old but robust, and he served them as guide and interpreter. When they returned in 1524, Pêro and his wife and family accompanied them for part of the way, and he sent his 23-year-old son with Dom Rodrigo to be educated in Portugal.

VASCO DA GAMA

(b. c. 1460, Sines, Portugal—d. December 24, 1524, Cochin [now Kochi], India)

Vasco da Gama, 1er conde da Vidigueira, was a Portuguese navigator who led three pivotal voyages to India (1497–99, 1502–03, 1524) that opened up the sea route from western Europe to South Asia by way of the Cape of Good Hope. With his first journey, he completed the series of explorations started some two decades earlier by Diogo Cão, who in the 1480s had reached the west and southwest coasts of Africa, and by Bartolomeu Dias, who led the expedition that discovered the Cape in 1488.

Little is known of Vasco's early life. He was the third son of Estêvão da Gama, a minor provincial nobleman who was commander of the fortress of Sines on the coast of Alentejo province in southwestern Portugal. In 1492 King John II of Portugal sent him to the port of Setúbal, south of Lisbon, and to the Algarve, Portugal's southernmost province, to seize French ships in retaliation for French peacetime depredations against Portuguese shipping—a task that da Gama rapidly and effectively performed.

John II died in 1495, and his cousin ascended the throne as Manuel I. The balance of power between factions at the Portuguese court then shifted in favour of friends and patrons of the da Gama family. Also at that time, Manuel revived the project initiated by his predecessor of sending a Portuguese fleet to India to open the sea route to Asia. By accomplishing this the Portuguese would outflank the Muslims, who controlled the eastern land routes and had hitherto enjoyed a monopoly of trade with India and beyond. For unknown reasons, da Gama, who had little relevant experience, was appointed to lead the expedition.

DA GAMA'S PIONEERING FIRST VOYAGE

Da Gama assembled a fleet of four vessels—two medium-sized three-masted sailing ships, each of about 120 tons, named the *São Gabriel* and the *São Rafael*; a 50-ton caravel, named the *Berrio*; and a 200-ton storeship. With da Gama's expedition went three interpreters — two Arabic speakers and one who spoke several Bantu dialects. He also carried stone pillars (*padrões*) that had been used since the time of Diogo Cão as markers of discovery and of Portuguese territorial claims. The fleet sailed from Lisbon on July 8, 1497.

The expedition passed the Canary Islands on July 15 and reached São Tiago in the Cape Verde Islands on the 26th, remaining there until August 3. Then, to avoid the currents of the Gulf of Guinea, da Gama undertook a long detour away from the African coast through the South Atlantic before attempting to round the Cape of Good Hope. The fleet reached Santa Helena Bay (in present-day South Africa) on November 7. Unfavourable winds and the adverse current there delayed the rounding of the Cape of Good Hope until November 22. Three days later da Gama anchored in Mossel Bay, erected a *padrão* on an island, and ordered the storeship to be broken up. Sailing again on December 8, the fleet reached the coast of what is now KwaZulu-Natal province on Christmas Day. On January 11, 1498, it anchored for five days near the mouth of a small river between Natal and present-day Mozambique, which they called the Rio do Cobre ("Copper River"). On January 25, farther north along the coast in Mozambique, they reached a stream that they called the Rio dos Bons Sinais ("River of Good Omens"; now the Bon Sinais River) and erected another *padrão*. By that time many of the crews were sick with scurvy; the expedition rested there a month while the ships were repaired.

On March 2 the fleet reached the Island of Mozambique, the inhabitants of which believed the Portuguese to be Muslims like themselves. Da Gama learned that they traded with Arab merchants and that four Arab vessels laden with gold, jewels, silver, and spices were then in port; he was also told that Prester John, the long-sought Christian ruler, lived

Da Gama kneeling before the zamorin of Calicut in India.
Hulton Archive/Getty Images

in the interior but held many coastal cities. The sultan of Mozambique supplied da Gama with two pilots, one of whom deserted when he discovered that the Portuguese were Christians.

The expedition reached Mombasa (now in Kenya) on April 7 and dropped anchor at Malindi (also now in Kenya) on April 14, where a pilot from Gujarat in India, who knew the route to Calicut (now Kozhikode), on the southwest coast of the subcontinent, was taken aboard. After a 23-day run across the Indian Ocean, the Western Ghats mountains of India were sighted, and Calicut was reached on May 20. There da Gama erected a *padrão* to prove he had reached India. The welcome of the *zamorin*, the Hindu ruler, of Calicut (then the most important trading centre of southern India), was dispelled by da Gama's insignificant gifts and rude behaviour. Da Gama failed to conclude a treaty— partly because of the hostility of Muslim merchants and partly because the trumpery presents and cheap trade goods that he had brought, while suited to the West African trade, were hardly in demand in India. The Portuguese had mistakenly believed the Hindus to be Christians.

After tension increased, da Gama left at the end of August, taking with him five or six Hindus so that King Manuel might learn about their customs. Ignorance and indifference to local knowledge had led da Gama to choose the worst possible time of year for his departure, and he had to sail against the summer monsoon. He visited Anjidiv Island (near Goa) before sailing for Malindi, which he reached on January 8, 1499, after nearly three months crossing the Arabian Sea. Many of the crew died of scurvy. At Malindi, because of greatly reduced numbers, da Gama ordered the São Rafael to be burned; there he also erected a *padrão*. Mozambique, where he set up his last *padrão*, was reached on February 1. On March 20 the São Gabriel and Berrio rounded the Cape together but a month later were parted by a storm; the Berrio reached the Tagus River in Portugal on July 10. Da Gama, in the São Gabriel, continued to Terceira Island in the Azores, whence he is said to have dispatched his flagship to Lisbon. He himself reached Lisbon on September 9 and made his triumphal entry nine days later, spending the interval mourning his brother Paulo, who had died on Terceira. (Out of da Gama's original crew of 170, only 55 men had survived.) Manuel I granted da Gama the title of dom, an annual pension of 1,000 cruzados, and estates.

THE SECOND VOYAGE

To exploit da Gama's achievement, Manuel I dispatched the Portuguese navigator Pedro Álvares Cabral to Calicut with a fleet of 13 ships. The profits of this expedition were such that a third fleet was soon fitted out in Lisbon. The command of this fleet was given to da Gama, who in January 1502 received the title of admiral. Da Gama commanded 10 ships, which were in turn supported by two flotillas of five ships each, each flotilla being under the command of one of his relations. Sailing in February 1502, the fleet called at the Cape Verdes, reaching the port of Sofala in East Africa on June 14. After calling briefly at Mozambique, the Portuguese expedition sailed to Kilwa, in what is now Tanzania. The ruler of Kilwa, the amīr Ibrāhīm, had been unfriendly to Cabral; da Gama threatened to burn Kilwa if the amīr did not submit to the Portuguese and swear loyalty to King Manuel, which he then did.

Coasting southern Arabia, da Gama then called at Goa (later the focus of Portuguese power in India) before proceeding to Cannanore (now Kannur), a port in south-western India to the north of Calicut, where he lay in wait for Arab shipping. After several days an Arab ship arrived with merchandise and between 200 and 400 passengers, including women and children. After seizing the cargo, da Gama is said to have shut up the passengers aboard the captured ship and set it afire, killing all on board. As a consequence, da Gama has been vilified, and Portuguese trading methods have been associated with terror. However, the episode is related only by late and unreliable sources and may be legendary or at least exaggerated.

After da Gama formed an alliance with the ruler of Cannanore—who was an enemy of the zamorin—the fleet sailed to Calicut, with the aim of wrecking its trade and punishing the *zamorin* for the favour he had shown to Muslim traders. Da Gama bombarded the port and seized and massacred 38 hostages. The Portuguese then sailed south to the port of Cochin, with whose ruler (also an enemy of the zamorin) they formed an alliance. After an invitation to da Gama from the *zamorin* had proved to be an attempt to entrap him, the Portuguese had a brief fight with Arab ships off Calicut but put them to full flight. On February 20, 1503, the fleet left Cannanore for Mozambique on the first stage of their return voyage, reaching the Tagus on October 11.

THE THIRD VOYAGE

Obscurity surrounds the reception of da Gama on his return by King Manuel. Da Gama seemingly felt himself inadequately recompensed for his pains. Controversy broke out between the admiral and the Order of São Tiago over the ownership of the town of Sines, which the admiral had been promised but which the order refused to yield. Da Gama had married a lady of good family, Caterina de Ataíde—perhaps in 1500 after his return from his first voyage—and he then appears to have retired to the town of Évora. He was later granted additional privileges and revenues, and his wife bore him six sons. Until 1505 he continued to advise the king on Indian matters, and he was created count of Vidigueira in 1519. Not until after King Manuel died was he again sent overseas; King John III nominated him in 1524 as Portuguese viceroy in India.

Arriving in Goa in September 1524, da Gama immediately set himself to correct the many administrative abuses that had crept in under his predecessors. Whether from overwork or other causes, he soon fell ill and died in Cochin in December. In 1538 his body was taken back to Portugal.

JUAN PONCE DE LEÓN

(b. 1460, Tierra de Campos Palencia, Leon
[Spain]—d. 1521, Havana [Cuba])

The Spanish explorer Juan Ponce de León founded the oldest settlement in Puerto Rico and later discovered Florida (1513) while searching for the mythical fountain of youth.

Born into a noble family, Ponce de León was a page in the royal court of Aragon and later fought in a campaign against the Moors in Granada. It is possible that he began his career of exploration in 1493 as part of Christopher Columbus' second expedition to the New World. In 1502 he was in the West Indies as a captain serving under Nicolás de Ovando, governor of Hispaniola. As a reward for suppressing an Indian mutiny, Ponce de León was named by Ovando to be the provincial governor of the eastern part of Hispaniola. Hearing persistent reports of gold to be found on Puerto Rico, Ponce de León in 1508–09 explored and settled that island, founding the colony's oldest settlement, Caparra, near what is now San Juan. He then returned to Hispaniola and was named governor of Puerto Rico but was soon displaced from the governorship through the political maneuvering of rivals.

The Spanish crown encouraged Ponce de León to continue searching for new lands. He learned from Indians of an island called Bimini (in the Bahamas) on which there was a miraculous spring or fountain that could rejuvenate those who drank from it (the fountain of youth). In search

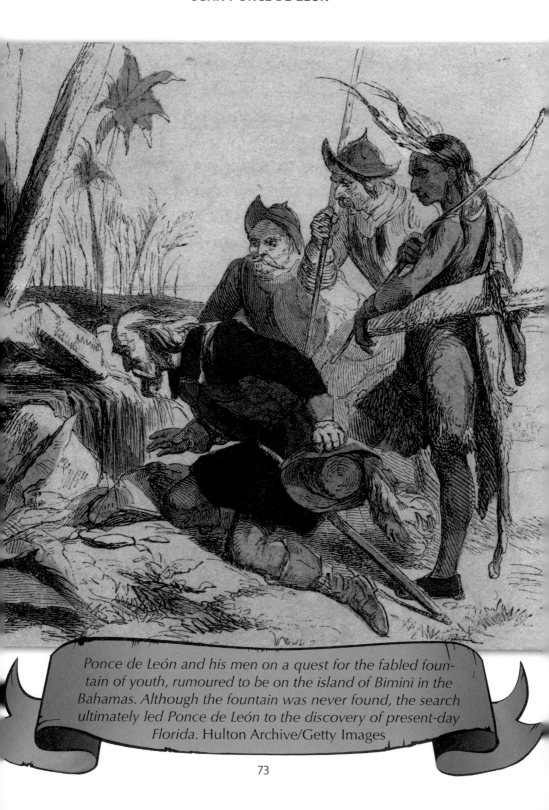

Ponce de León and his men on a quest for the fabled fountain of youth, rumoured to be on the island of Bimini in the Bahamas. Although the fountain was never found, the search ultimately led Ponce de León to the discovery of present-day Florida. Hulton Archive/Getty Images

of this fountain, he led a privately outfitted expedition from Puerto Rico in March 1513 and in April of that year landed on the coast of Florida near the site of modern St. Augustine. At the time he did not realize that he was on the mainland of North America and instead supposed he had landed on an island. He named the region Florida because it was discovered at Easter time (Spanish: Pascua Florida) and because it abounded in lush, florid vegetation. He coasted southward, sailing through the Florida Keys and ending his search near Charlotte Harbor on Florida's west coast. He then returned to Puerto Rico and thence to Spain, where he secured the title in 1514 of military governor of Bimini and Florida with permission to colonize those regions.

In 1521 Ponce de León sailed again for Florida with two ships and 200 men, landing near Charlotte Harbor. On this occasion he was wounded by an arrow during an Indian attack, and he died after being returned to Cuba. Puerto Rico's third largest city, Ponce, is named in his honour.

DIEGO VELÁZQUEZ DE CUÉLLAR

(b. c. 1465, Cuéllar, Spain—d. 1524, Santiago de Cuba, Cuba)

The conquistador Diego Velázquez de Cuéllar was the first Spanish governor of Cuba. He sailed to the New World in 1493 on the second voyage of Christopher Columbus. Columbus' eldest son, Diego Columbus, later entrusted Velázquez with the conquest of Cuba under the title of adelantado (governor) and, with Hernán Cortés,

Velázquez departed for Cuba in 1511. In the next four years he founded the settlements of Baracoa, Bayamo, Santiago de Cuba, and Havana (La Habana). After his conquests were completed about 1514, he encouraged colonization and became governor of Cuba.

Velázquez organized the exploration of the coasts of the Yucatán Peninsula and the Gulf of Mexico led by Hernández de Córdoba (1517) and Juan de Grijalba (1518), and in 1518 he appointed Cortés leader of a new expedition to conquer the mainland of Mexico. Velázquez subsequently became suspicious of the independent-minded Cortés and rescinded the order; Cortés sailed without permission in 1519, and Velázquez sent two unsuccessful expeditions against him. One was so badly defeated that its commander, Pánfilo de Narváez, and his army went over to the side of Cortés.

Velázquez complained to the Spanish court, but, after Aztec riches started to arrive from Mexico, he was instructed to ignore Cortés.

PEDRO ÁLVARES CABRAL

(b. 1467/68, Belmonte, Portugal—d. 1520, Santarém?)

The Portuguese navigator and explorer Pedro Álvares Cabral led the maritime voyage in 1500 that is generally credited with discovering Brazil (April 22). His expedition also became only the second from Europe (after Vasco da Gama had done so in 1498) to reach India via the sea route around the Cape of Good Hope.

He was the son of Fernão Cabral, a nobleman, and of Isabel de Gouveia and was heir to a long tradition of service to the throne. Cabral himself was favoured by King Manuel I of Portugal who bestowed a number of privileges on Cabral in 1497, including a personal allowance, the title of counselor to his highness, and the habit of the military Order of Christ. Following up on da Gama's pioneering voyage, in 1500 Manuel, expressing his great confidence in Cabral's leadership, gave Cabral command of the important next maritime mission to India. Made an admiral, Cabral set out from Lisbon on March 9, 1500, with a fleet of 13 ships and orders to follow the earlier route of da Gama, strengthen commercial ties, and further the conquest his predecessor had begun.

In accordance with da Gama's instructions, based on his experiences during the first voyage, Cabral was to sail southwest so as to bypass the becalmed waters of the Gulf of Guinea. This course, which later became known as the "circle around Brazil," had the added advantage of providing the Portuguese with opportunity to reconnoitre along the coast of the lands to the west, which they had previously sighted and which belonged to them in accordance with the Treaty of Tordesillas (1494) that divided the still almost completely unknown New World between Spain and Portugal.

The fleet sailed westward under favourable conditions, and on April 22 Cabral sighted the land he named Island of the True Cross. Later renamed Holy Cross by King Manuel, the country ultimately took its modern name, Brazil, from a kind of dyewood, *pau-brasil*, that is found there.

Cabral is reported to have made a special effort to treat the inhabitants kindly, receiving them on board his caravel. Nonetheless, he took formal possession of the country and dispatched one of his ships to Portugal to

Cabral claiming Brazil for Portugal.
Apic/Hulton Archive/Getty Images

inform the king. Henceforth, maps of the region showed Portugal as ruler of a great expanse of land with vaguely defined boundaries that came to serve as a point of call on the long voyage from Europe to the Cape of Good Hope and the Indian Ocean.

After a stay of only 10 days in Brazil, Cabral sailed for India, in a voyage that was plagued by a series of misfortunes. On May 29, while the fleet was rounding the Cape of Good Hope, four ships were lost with all hands aboard. The remaining ships cast anchor on September 13, 1500, at Calicut (now Kozhikode), India, where the *zamorin* (the Hindu ruler of Calicut) welcomed Cabral and allowed him to establish a fortified trading post. Disputes with Muslim traders soon arose, however, and on December 17 a large Muslim force attacked the trading post. Most of the Portuguese defenders were killed before reinforcements could arrive from the Portuguese fleet lying at anchor in the harbour.

Cabral retaliated by bombarding the city, and then by capturing 10 Muslim vessels and executing their crews. He then sailed for the Indian port of Cochin (now Kochi), farther south, where he was affably received and permitted to trade for precious spices, with which he loaded his six remaining ships. Cabral also made port at Carangolos and Cananor on the same coast, completed his cargo, and on January 16, 1501, began the return voyage to Portugal. On his way, however, two ships foundered, and it was with only four vessels that Cabral finally reached the mouth of the Tagus River in Portugal on June 23, 1501.

King Manuel was pleased at the outcome of the undertaking, in spite of the misfortunes that had beset it; he is said to have at first favoured making Cabral head of a new and more powerful expedition, but in the end it was Vasco da Gama and not Cabral who was appointed to that command. Accounts differ as to the reason for the king's change of heart. One chronicler attributes it to disagreement over division of authority within the new fleet; another offers the explanation that da Gama opposed the appointment of Cabral on the grounds that da Gama himself already held the title admiral of all the fleets that might leave Portugal for India and that the disasters of Cabral's expedition should disqualify him for the new mission.

Whatever the true explanation, Cabral held no further position of authority at the Portuguese court. He retired to his estate in the Beira Baixa province of Portugal and spent his remaining years there. His tomb at Santarém was identified in 1848 by the Brazilian historian Francisco Adolfo Varnhagen.

In 1968, the year that marked the fifth centenary of the birth of Cabral, Brazil and Portugal honoured the memory of the "admiral of the fleet" in joint festivities. Both Rio de Janeiro and Lisbon have erected monuments in his honour.

JOÃO DA NOVA

(b. 15th century, Galicia, Spain—d. 1509, Cochin
[now Kozhikode], India)

João da Nova (Spanish: Juan de Nova) was a Spanish navigator who, in the service of Portugal, discovered the Atlantic Ocean islands of Ascension and St. Helena, both off the southwestern coast of Africa. Commanding a fleet of four ships, he left Portugal on a voyage to India in 1501. En route he discovered Ascension Island. In India he established a trading post at Cannanore (now Kannur). During his return voyage to Portugal, Nova discovered St. Helena.

After returning to India, Nova had a falling-out with Francisco de Almeida and Afonso de Albuquerque, who were rivals for leadership of the Estado da India (Portuguese-held India).

LODOVICO DE VARTHEMA

(b. c. 1465–70, Bologna [Italy]—d. June 1517, Rome, Papal States)

Lodovico de Varthema (or di Barthema, Latin: Vartomanus or Vertomannus) was an intrepid Italian traveler and adventurer whose account of his Middle Eastern and Asiatic wanderings was widely circulated throughout Europe and earned him high fame in his own lifetime. He made significant discoveries (especially in Arabia) and made many valuable observations of the peoples he visited; his ready wit enabled him to handle difficult situations.

Varthema sailed from Venice near the end of 1502, visited Alexandria and Cairo, proceeded up the Syrian coast, and went inland to Damascus. Then, either adopting Islam or pretending to, he became the first Christian known to have made the *hajj* (holy pilgrimage) to Mecca, a journey of gravest danger for a non-Muslim. He completed the trip between April and June 1503 and remained in Mecca about three weeks. In his writings he provides an accurate description of both the town and the religious rituals practiced there. Deserting his Syrian caravan, he then joined a group of Indian pilgrims on their way to India. He was, however, arrested as a Christian spy at Aden and imprisoned for two months. Sent to the palace of the sultan, Varthema gained the intercession of one of the sultan's wives. By this means, and by feigning madness, he was set free. He then made a walking tour of about 600 miles (965 km) through the mountainous southwestern corner of the Arabian peninsula, visiting Sanaa, Yemen.

Varthema next sailed for northwestern India by way of Somaliland but then returned to Arabia. Touching at Ẓupār and Muscat, he went on to Hormuz in the Persian Gulf and spent much of 1504 in southern Persia. At Shīrāz, Persia, he entered into partnership with a merchant whom he knew from his Mecca pilgrimage and who accompanied him on the rest of his Asian travels. Following an unsuccessful attempt to reach Samarkand, the two men returned to Hormuz and embarked for India. Sailing the length of the western coast, they touched at Cambay (now Khambhat) and at Goa, from where Varthema visited the inland capital of Bijapur; at Cannanore (now Kannur) he detoured to visit Vijayanagar (now Hampi), a great city enjoying its final days of splendour; at Calicut (now Kozhikode) Varthema observed Hindu customs as well as trade and city government. He visited Ceylon (now Sri Lanka) and southeastern India and then made his way to the magnificent Myanmar (Burmese) capital at Pegu. From Malacca (now Melaka), on the southern Malay peninsula, he returned to India in the summer of 1505 and, upon reaching Calicut, posed as a Muslim holy man. Eager to return to Europe, Varthema joined the Portuguese garrison at Cannanore, fought for Portugal, and was knighted for his services. In 1507 he sailed for Europe by way of the Cape of Good Hope.

Varthema's account, *Itinerario de Ludouico de Varthema Bolognese...* (1510), first appeared in English translation in Richard Eden's *History of Travayle* (1576–77). The Hakluyt Society of London published an English translation, *Travels of Ludovico di Varthema*, in 1863.

DIEGO DE ALMAGRO

(b. 1475, Almagro, Castile [Spain]—d. 1538, Cuzco, Peru)

The Spanish soldier Diego de Almagro played a leading role in the Spanish conquest of Peru. Following service in the Spanish navy, Almagro arrived in South America in 1524 and, with his intimate friend Francisco Pizarro, led the expedition that conquered the Inca empire in what is now Peru. Almagro and Pizarro became joint captains general of these conquests, which the Spaniards called New Castile. Bitter enmity soon arose between Almagro and Pizarro, however, leading to much political instability in the new colony.

In 1534 King Charles I of Spain (also Holy Roman emperor as Charles V) sent Almagro to assist in the conquest of what is now Chile, where he is said to have suffered great hardships. During Almagro's absence, Indians in Peru rebelled and even besieged the Spanish fortress of Cuzco. Almagro rushed back to Peru, put down the insurrection, and then imprisoned Pizarro's two brothers Hernando and Alonso for having refused to obey his orders during the fighting. This brought

Francisco Pizarro to Cuzco, where he defeated Almagro's army, captured Almagro, and put him to death in the first of several internecine wars between the Spanish captains in the new colony.

LOURENÇO DE ALMEIDA

(d. 1508, Chaul, India)

The Portuguese sea captain Lourenço de Almeida was the leader of a 1505 expedition to Ceylon (now Sri Lanka), probably the first Portuguese voyage to that island. He was the son of Francisco de Almeida, the first viceroy of Portuguese India (1505–09). Lourenço had been sent by his father to explore the Maldives, to establish alliances, and to form trade relations. Almeida brought Portuguese influence to the region, founding a settlement at Colombo in 1505.

The deflection of Arab and Egyptian trade brought conflict. Almeida defeated an Arab fleet off the west coast of India in 1506 and a fleet from Malacca (now Melaka) in 1508 near Chaul. There, however, he was trapped by an Egyptian armada. He fought with bravery, and his exploits were later celebrated by the 16th-century Portuguese poet Camões in his patriotic epic poem *Os Lusíadas (The Lusiads*, referring to the ancient Roman territory, Lusitania, that embraced what became Portugal). Almeida died of wounds received in the battle. Two years later the Portuguese scattered a combined Turkish and Muslim fleet near the port of Diu, finally establishing Portuguese power in much of the territory east of Suez.

VASCO NÚÑEZ DE BALBOA

(b. 1475, Jerez de los Caballeros, or Badajoz,
Extremadura province, Castile—d. January 12,
1519, Acla, near Darién, Panama),

The Spanish conquistador and explorer Vasco Núñez de Balboa was head of the first stable settlement on the South American continent (1511) and was the first European to sight the Pacific Ocean (September 25 [or 27], 1513).

CAREER IN THE NEW WORLD

Balboa came from the ranks of that lower nobility whose sons—"men of good family who were not reared behind the plow," in the words of the chronicler Gonzalo Fernández de Oviedo y Valdés—often sought their fortunes in the Indies. In 1500 he sailed with Rodrigo de Bastidas on a voyage of exploration along the coast of present-day Colombia. Later, he settled in Hispaniola (Haiti), but he did not prosper as a pioneer farmer and had to escape his creditors by embarking as a stowaway on an expedition organized by Martín Fernández de Enciso (1510) to bring aid and reinforcements to a colony founded by Alonso de Ojeda on the coast of Urabá, in modern Colombia. The expedition found the survivors of the colony, led by Francisco Pizarro, but Ojeda had departed. On the advice of Balboa the settlers moved across the Gulf of

Urabá to Darién, on the less hostile coast of the Isthmus
of Panama, where they founded the town of Santa María
de la Antigua, the first stable settlement on the continent,
and began to acquire gold by barter or war with the local
Indians. The colonists soon deposed Enciso, Ojeda's second in command, and elected a town council; one of its
two alcaldes, or magistrates, was Balboa. With the subsequent departure of Enciso for Hispaniola, Balboa became
the undisputed head of the colony. In December 1511 King
Ferdinand II sent orders that named Balboa interim governor and captain general of Darién.

Balboa meanwhile had organized a series of gold- and
slave-hunting expeditions into the Indian chiefdoms of
the area. His Indian policy combined the use of barter,
every kind of force, including torture, to extract information, and the tactic of divide and conquer by forming
alliances with certain tribes against others. The Indians of
Darién, less warlike than their neighbours of Urabá and
without poisoned arrows, were not formidable foes and
often fled at the approach of the Spaniards. The Spanish
arsenal included their terrible war dogs, sometimes used
by Balboa as executioners to tear Indian victims to pieces.

The Spaniards were told by Indians that to the south lay
a sea and a province infinitely rich in gold—a reference to
the Pacific and perhaps to the Inca Empire. The conquest
of that land, their informants declared, would require 1,000
men. Balboa hastened to send emissaries to Spain to request
reinforcements; the news they brought created much excitement, and a large expedition was promptly organized. But
Balboa was not given command. Charges brought against
him by his enemies had turned King Ferdinand against
him, and he sent out the elderly, powerful nobleman Pedro
Arias Dávila (usually called Pedrarias) as commander of the
armada and governor of Darién. The expedition, number-
ing 2,000 persons, left Spain in April 1514.

DISCOVERY OF THE PACIFIC

Meanwhile, Balboa, without waiting for reinforcements, had sailed on September 1, 1513, from Santa María for Acla, at the narrowest part of the isthmus. Accompanied by 190 Spaniards and hundreds of Indian carriers, he marched south across the isthmus through dense jungles, rivers, and swamps and ascended the cordillera; on September 25 (or 27), 1513, standing "silent, upon a peak in Darién," he sighted the Pacific. Some days later he reached the shore of the Gulf of San Miguel and took possession of the Mar del Sur (South Sea) and the adjacent lands for the king of Castile. He then recrossed the isthmus, arriving at Santa María in January 1514. His letters and those of a royal agent who had been sent to Darién to prepare the ground for the coming of Pedrarias, announcing the discovery of the "South Sea," restored Balboa to royal favour; he was named *adelantado* (governor) of the Mar del Sur and of the provinces of Panamá and Coiba but remained subject to the authority of Pedrarias, who arrived in Darién, now a crown colony and renamed Castilla del Oro, in June 1514.

Relations between the two men were, from the first, troubled by the distrust and jealousy of the ailing, ill-natured Pedrarias toward the younger man. The first bishop of Darién, Juan de Quevedo, sought to act as peacemaker and arranged a temporary reconciliation; in a turnabout Pedrarias by proxy betrothed his daughter María in Spain to Balboa. But the underlying causes of friction remained. The suspicious Pedrarias pursued a tortuous policy designed to frustrate Balboa at every turn; but he at last gave Balboa grudging permission to explore the South Sea. By dint of enormous efforts Balboa had a fleet of ships built and transported in pieces across the mountains to the Pacific shore, where he explored the Gulf of San Miguel (1517–18).

Balboa and his men sighting the Pacific Ocean for the first time. Hulton Archive/Getty Images

Meantime, the stream of charges of misconduct and incapacity leveled against Pedrarias by Balboa and others had finally convinced the crown of Pedrarias' unfitness to govern; news arrived in Darién of his imminent replacement by a new governor who would subject Pedrarias to a *residencia* (judicial review of his conduct in office). Pedrarias doubtless feared that Balboa's presence and testimony would contribute to his total ruin and decided to get rid of his rival. Summoned home on the pretext that Pedrarias wished to discuss matters of common concern, Balboa was seized and charged with rebellion, high treason, and mistreatment of Indians, among other misdeeds. After a farcical trial presided over by Gaspar de Espinosa, Pedrarias' chief justice, Balboa was found guilty, condemned to death, and beheaded with four alleged accomplices in January 1519.

FRANCISCO PIZARRO

(b. c. 1475, Trujillo, Extremadura, Castile [Spain]—d. June 26, 1541, Lima [now in Peru])

The Spanish conquistador Francisco Pizarro was the conqueror of the Inca empire and founder of the city of Lima, Peru.

EARLY LIFE

Pizarro was the illegitimate son of Captain Gonzalo Pizarro and Francisca González, a young girl of humble

Francisco Pizarro, undated engraving.
Library of Congress, Washington, D.C.

birth. He spent much of his early life in the home of his grandparents. According to legend he was for a time a swineherd, a not unlikely possibility since this was a common occupation of boys in that region. He doubtless participated in local manorial wars and, when these were ended, very probably went to fight in Italy. Certainly in 1502 he went to Hispaniola (modern Haiti and Dominican Republic) with the new governor of the Spanish colony.

Pizarro had little inclination toward the settled life of the colonizer, and in 1510 he enrolled in an expedition of the explorer Alonso de Ojeda to Urabá in Colombia. He appears to have been marked out as a hard, silent, and apparently unambitious man who could be trusted in difficult situations. Three years later, acting as captain, he participated in an expedition led by the explorer Vasco Núñez de Balboa that was credited with the European discovery of the Pacific. From 1519 to 1523 he was mayor and magistrate of the newly founded town of Panamá, accumulating a small fortune.

DISCOVERY AND CONQUEST OF PERU

It was not until 1523, when he was some 48 years old, that Pizarro embarked upon the adventure that was to lead to his lasting fame. In partnership with a soldier, Diego de Almagro, and a priest, Hernando de Luque, he made preparations for a voyage of discovery and conquest down the west coast of South America. Many hardships were endured along the Colombian coast during the first (1524–25) and second (1526–28) expeditions. Bartolomé Ruiz, who joined Pizarro and Almagro for the latter, sailed ahead and crossed the Equator, encountering a trading raft carrying embroidered fabrics and precious metals from Peru. He returned and led the expedition as far south as Ecuador. Pizarro and others remained on coastal islands while Almagro was sent back to Panama for reinforcements. The new governor of Panama, however, sent back orders that the expedition be abandoned in order that no more lives be lost. At this point Pizarro is reputed to have drawn a line on the ground with his sword, inviting those who desired wealth and glory to cross it. The "famous thirteen" who did cross the line continued their exploration of the coast as far as latitude 9° S, obtaining distinct accounts of a great Indian empire as well as many Inca artifacts. They christened the new land Peru, probably a corruption of Virú, the name of a river.

Finding the governor of Panama still opposed to their now promising enterprise, the explorers decided that Pizarro should go to Spain to ask the Holy Roman emperor Charles V (Charles I of Spain) for permission to undertake conquest. Sailing in the spring of 1528, Pizarro was in Sevilla (Seville) at the same time as Hernán Cortés, conqueror of Mexico, and was able to win Charles over to his scheme. He was decorated, granted a coat of arms, and, in July 1529, made governor and captain general of the province of New Castile for a distance 600 miles (965 km) south of Panama along the newly discovered coast. Pizarro was invested with all the authority and prerogatives of a viceroy, and Almagro and Luque were left in subordinate positions. All the "famous thirteen" received substantial rights and privileges in the new territories.

Joined by four of his brothers, Pizarro sailed for Panama in January 1530 and by January of the following year was ready to set off for Peru. He set sail with one ship, 180 men, and 37 horses, being joined later by two more ships. By April they had made contact with emissaries of Atahuallpa, emperor of the Incas, who was residing near the city of Cajamarca with an army of about 30,000 men. Somewhat scornful of Pizarro's small force, the Inca accepted a proposal that the two leaders meet in that city.

Arriving on November 15, Pizarro immediately set up his artillery and sent his brother Hernando and another Spaniard to request an interview. After a day of tense waiting, Atahuallpa, borne on a litter, entered the great square of Cajamarca with an escort of between 3,000 and 4,000 men, who were either unarmed or carrying short clubs and slings beneath their tunics. Pizarro sent out a priest, Vicente de Valverde, to exhort the Inca to accept Christianity and Charles V as his master. Atahuallpa disputed both the religion and the sovereignty of the Spaniards and, after examining a Bible offered by the priest, flung the book to the ground. Valverde reported these events to Pizarro, who immediately ordered an attack. The astonished Incas were cut down from all sides, Pizarro himself seizing Atahuallpa.

Atahuallpa was held as hostage and failed to win his release, though he fulfilled a promise to fill the chamber in which he was held with gold and silver. Accused of ordering the execution of his brother Huascar, a rival for the title of Inca (ruler), and of plotting to overthrow the Spaniards, Atahuallpa was put to death by strangulation on Aug. 29, 1533. With news of Atahuallpa's death, the Inca armies surrounding Cajamarca retreated, and Pizarro progressed toward Cuzco, the royal capital, which was occupied without a struggle in November 1533. The Spaniards declared Manco Capac, Huascar's brother, as Inca.

For the remainder of his life, Pizarro was engaged in consolidating the Spanish hold on Peru and in defending his and his brothers' share of the spoils. A certain enmity and rivalry developed between him and Almagro as a result of Pizarro's overriding powers from the king of Spain. This contravened a solemn agreement between the original three partners that the spoils of the expedition should be shared equally. Almagro at one stage seized Cuzco but was persuaded by Pizarro to depart for Chile, over which he had been granted extensive powers by the king. Disappointed by the poverty of that country, however, he returned to Peru, where he was made prisoner and later executed by Hernando Pizarro.

Francisco Pizarro, meanwhile, was in Lima, a city that he had founded in 1535 and to which he devoted the last two years of his life. Almagro's former adherents had grouped around Almagro's son in Lima, where they were confined and watched. Suspecting that they were to be eliminated, they decided to move first, attacking Pizarro's palace on June 26, 1541. Pizarro died that day a protracted death, drawing a cross of his own blood on the ground, kissing it, and crying "Jesus" as he fell.

SEBASTIAN CABOT

(b. c. 1476, Bristol, Gloucestershire, England, or Venice [Italy]—d. 1557, London)

Sebastian Cabot was a son of the Italian-born English navigator and explorer John Cabot, who led the first two English expeditions (1497 and 1498, respectively) to North America. Sebastian himself was also a navigator and explorer, as well as a cartographer, who at various times served the English and Spanish crowns.

Facts about Cabot's early life remain obscure. He may have accompanied his father on the 1497 North American voyage, which resulted in the discovery of the Labrador coast of Newfoundland (mistaken at the time for the coast of China). Cabot was a cartographer to King Henry VIII in 1512, when he accompanied the English army sent to aid King Ferdinand II of Aragon against the French. Because of his knowledge of the northeast coast of North America, he was commissioned a captain in the Spanish navy, but Ferdinand's death canceled a voyage he was to command in 1516. His services were retained by the Holy Roman emperor Charles V, and in 1518 he was given membership in the Spanish Casa de las Indias ("House of the Indies") and appointed *piloto mayor* (master navigator), a position of great importance (once held by Amerigo Vespucci) whose duties included being official examiner of pilots and the cartographer maintaining for the crown all records and maps of maritime routes and newly discovered lands.

Cabot returned to England in 1520 and was offered a naval command, but in 1525 he assumed charge of a three-ship Spanish expedition that was to develop maritime trade with Asia. He diverted the expedition from this objective, however, because of reports of fabulous wealth in the Río de la Plata region of South America. After about three years of fruitless exploration he returned to Spain, was judged responsible for the failure of the expedition, and was banished to Africa. Pardoned two years later, he was restored to his old post of piloto mayor. A copy of his well-known map of the world (1544) is in the Bibliothèque Nationale, Paris.

Offered a naval post in England by King Edward VI, Cabot accepted the appointment (1548) and was also pensioned. He remained in England as governor of the Merchant Adventurers, organizing an expedition to search for a northeast passage from Europe to East Asia. Although this objective was not attained, and several naval disasters ensued, the voyage did facilitate trade with Russia.

JUAN SEBASTIÁN DEL CANO

(b. c. 1476, Guetaria, Vizcaya, Castile [now Spain]—d. August 4, 1526, at sea)

The Basque navigator and explorer Juan Sebastián del Cano (or Elcano) is credited for having completed the first circumnavigation of Earth. He accomplished this as part of the famous expedition led by Ferdinand Magellan.

Juan Sebastián del Cano. Bjorn Landstrom/National Geographic Image Collection/Getty Images

Cano was master of the *Concepción*, one of the five vessels in Magellan's Spanish-sponsored fleet that in September 1519 sailed west from Europe with the goal of reaching the Spice Islands (the Moluccas) in what is now Indonesia. After Magellan's death in the Philippines in April 1521, a series of men took command of the expedition in the two surviving ships, but none of them stayed in charge for longer than a few months. As one of the few remaining men, Cano finally took charge of the last surviving ship, the *Victoria*, later that year. He safely brought that vessel home to Spain in September 1522, despite the remaining crew being beset by scurvy, starvation, and harassment by the Portuguese. Only 18 Europeans had survived the voyage, which constituted the first journey around the globe.

In 1525 Cano was appointed chief pilot on García Jofre de Loaisa's expedition to claim the Moluccas for Spain. The expedition was ultimately a failure, though, and both Cano and Loaisa lost their lives.

FERDINAND MAGELLAN

(b. c. 1480, Sabrosa or Porto?, Portugal—d. April 27, 1521, Mactan, Philippines)

The renowned Portuguese navigator and explorer Ferdinand Magellan (Portuguese Fernão de Magalhães, Spanish Fernando de Magallanes) undertook numerous long-distance maritime voyages during a career of more than 15 years. He first sailed under the flag of Portugal (1505–13) before changing his allegiance to Spain,

Ferdinand Magellan, detail of a painting by an unknown artist; in the Uffizi Gallery, Florence. Alinari—Art Resource/EB, Inc.

for which he embarked on the famous around-the-world expedition of 1519–22. From Spain he led a fleet that sailed around South America—in the process discovering the Strait of Magellan—and across the Pacific Ocean. Though he was killed in the Philippines in 1521, one of his ships continued westward to Spain, arriving there the next year and accomplishing the first circumnavigation of Earth.

The voyage was successfully completed by the Basque navigator Juan Sebastián del Cano.

YEARS IN PORTUGUESE SERVICE

Magellan was from a privileged background: his father Rui de Magalhães and his mother Alda de Mesquita were members of the Portuguese nobility. He became a page in Lisbon to Queen Leonor, wife of John II (reigned 1481–95) and sister of Manuel I (reigned 1495–1521), when he was quite young. In early 1505 he enlisted in the fleet of Francisco de Almeida, first viceroy of Portuguese India, whose expedition King Manuel sent to check Muslim sea power along the African and Indian coasts and to establish a strong Portuguese presence in the Indian Ocean. During a naval engagement at Cannanore (now Kannur) on the Malabar Coast of India, Magellan is said by the chronicler Gaspar Correia (also spelled Corrêa) to have been wounded. Though Correia states that during this early period of his Indian service, Magellan acquired considerable knowledge of navigation, little is known of Magellan's first years in the East until he appears among those sailing in November 1506 with Nuno Vaz Pereira to Sofala on the Mozambique coast, where the Portuguese had established a fort.

By 1507 Magellan was back in India. He took part, on February 2–3, 1509, in the great Battle of Diu, in which the Portuguese defeated a Muslim fleet and thereby gained supremacy over most of the Indian Ocean. Reaching Cochin (now Kochi, India) in the fleet of Diogo Lopes de Sequeira, he subsequently left for the Malay city-state of Malacca (now Melaka, Malaysia). Magellan is mentioned as being sent to warn the commander of the Portuguese ships in Malacca's waters of impending attack by Malays.

During the subsequent fighting he saved the life of a Portuguese explorer, his close friend Francisco Serrão. (Serrão, possibly a relative of Magellan's, had sailed with Magellan to India in 1505.) Magellan attempted to return to Portugal afterward but was unsuccessful. At a council held at Cochin on October 10, 1510, to decide on plans for retaking Goa—which the Portuguese had captured earlier in the year but then lost—he advised against taking large ships at that season. Nevertheless, the new Portuguese governor in India, Afonso de Albuquerque, did so, and the city fell to the Portuguese on November 24. Magellan's name does not appear among those who fought.

The Portuguese victories off the eastern coast of Africa and the western coast of India had broken Muslim power in the Indian Ocean, and the purpose of Almeida's expedition—to wrest from the Arabs the key points of sea trade—was almost accomplished. Yet without control of Malacca, their achievement was incomplete. At the end of June 1511, therefore, a fleet under Albuquerque left for Malacca, which fell after six weeks. This event, in which Magellan took part, was the crowning Portuguese victory in the Orient. Through Malacca passed the wealth of the East to the harbours of the West, and in command of the Malacca Strait the Portuguese held the key to the seas and ports of Malaysia. It remained only to explore the wealth-giving Moluccas (now part of Indonesia), the islands of spice. Accordingly, early in December 1511 they sailed on a voyage of reconnaissance, and after reaching Banda they returned with spice in 1512. The claim made by some that Magellan went on this voyage rests on unproven statements by Italian geographer Giovanni Battista Ramusio and Spanish historian Leonardo de Argensola, and the want of evidence argues against its acceptance. However, it is known that Magellan's friend Serrão was in command of one of the ships and that he later sent Magellan helpful information from the Moluccas about those islands.

By mid-1513 Magellan was back in Lisbon, but he soon joined the forces sent against the Moroccan stronghold of Azamor (Azemmour). In a skirmish that August he sustained a leg wound that caused him to limp for the rest of his life. Returning to Lisbon in November 1514, he asked King Manuel for a token increase in his pension as a reward. But unfounded reports of irregular conduct on his part had reached the king: after the siege of Azamor, Magellan was accused of having sold a portion of the war spoils back to the enemy. Refusing Magellan's request for a reward, Manuel ordered him back to Morocco. Early in 1516 Magellan renewed his petition; the king, refusing once more, told him he might offer his services elsewhere.

SHIFTING OF ALLEGIANCE TO SPAIN

Magellan therefore went to Spain, reaching Sevilla (Seville) on October 20, 1517. He was joined in December by the Portuguese cosmographer Rui Faleiro and possibly by Rui's brother Francisco Faleiro. Magellan and Rui Faleiro journeyed to the court at Valladolid, where they offered their services to King Charles I (later, Holy Roman emperor Charles V). Magellan, until this point bearing the Portuguese name Fernão de Magalhães, henceforward became known by the Spanish version of his name — Fernando (or Hernando) de Magallanes.

By the Treaty of Tordesillas (1494), all newly discovered and undiscovered territories east of a line of demarcation (370 leagues west of the Cape Verde Islands) were assigned to Portugal; all that lay west belonged to Spain. Magellan and Faleiro now proposed to sail west to give practical

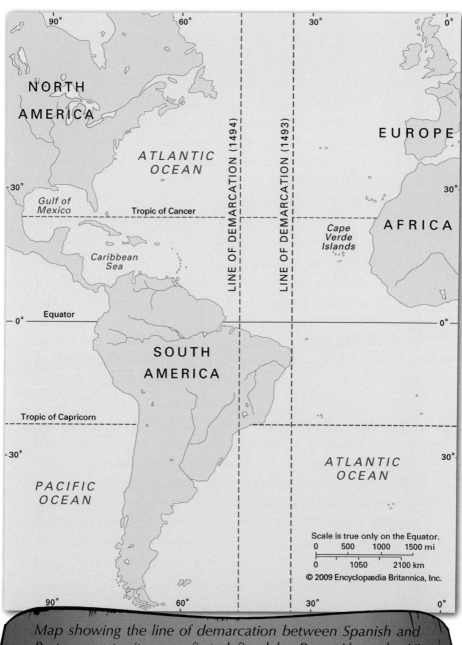

Map showing the line of demarcation between Spanish and Portuguese territory, as first defined by Pope Alexander VI (1493) and later revised by the Treaty of Tordesillas (1494). Spain won control of lands discovered west of the line, while Portugal gained rights to new lands to the east.

proof of their claim that the Spice Islands lay west of the line of demarcation—that is, within the Spanish, not the Portuguese, hemisphere. Magellan was convinced that he would lead his ships from the Atlantic to the "Sea of the South" by discovering a strait through Tierra Firme (the South American mainland). This idea did not originate with him; others had sought a passage by which vessels sailing continuously westward would reach the East and thus avoid the African Cape of Good Hope, which was controlled by the Portuguese.

On March 22, 1518, their proposal received royal assent. Magellan and Faleiro were appointed joint captains general of an expedition directed to seek an all-Spanish route to the Moluccas. In the royal agreement, Magellan and Faleiro were directed to find "the" strait, referring to the hypothetical passage through Tierra Firme. The government of any lands discovered was to be vested in them and their heirs, and they were to receive a one-twentieth share of the net profits from the venture. Both also were invested with the Order of Santiago, a Spanish military-religious knighthood.

The Spanish seafaring community reacted strongly against the king's acceptance of the Portuguese-led expedition. The influence of Juan Rodríguez de Fonseca, the bishop of Burgos and head of the powerful Casa de Contratación (House of Commerce), an administrative entity that oversaw all Spanish explorations, hindered the proper organization of the expedition, which was delayed more than once. Agents of the Portuguese crown, outraged by Magellan's transfer of allegiance, also made an unsuccessful attempt to wreck the project. Ultimately, the number of Portuguese sailors assigned to the expedition was strictly limited, Fonseca managed to install a Spanish officer as a sort of cocommander of the fleet, and Magellan lost his Portuguese cocaptain, Faleiro, whose mental instability prevented him from sailing. Conflicts between the Portuguese and Spanish officers on board were to lead to severe discipline problems during the voyage.

Spanish officials furnished five ships for the expedition, prepared in Sevilla. Magellan's flagship, the *Trinidad*, had as consorts the *San Antonio*, the *Concepción*, the *Victoria*, and the *Santiago*. The ships were old ones, not in the best condition or fitted as Magellan would have liked. Nevertheless, Magellan—who in 1517 had married Beatriz Barbosa, daughter of an important official in Sevilla—said farewell to his wife and infant son, Rodrigo, before his ships left Sanlúcar de Barrameda on September 20, 1519.

DISCOVERY OF THE STRAIT OF MAGELLAN

The fleet, carrying about 270 men, predominantly from Spain and Portugal but also from far-flung parts of Europe and North Africa, reached Tenerife in the Canary Islands on September 26, 1519, and set sail on October 3 for Brazil. Becalmed off the Guinea coast of Africa, it met storms before reaching the Equator; by November 29, having crossed the Atlantic successfully, it was 27 leagues southwest of Cape St. Augustine (Cabo de Santo Agostinho, Brazil). Rounding Cape Frio, Magellan entered the bay of Rio de Janeiro on December 13. He then sailed south to the Río de la Plata and vainly probed the estuary, seeking the strait. On March 31, 1520, he reached Port Saint Julian (San Julián, Argentina), where on Easter day at midnight Spanish captains led a serious mutiny against the Portuguese commander. With resolution, ruthlessness, and daring, Magellan quelled it: he executed one of the mutinous captains and left another to his fate ashore when, on August 24, 1520, the fleet left Saint Julian.

After reaching the mouth of the Santa Cruz River, near which the *Santiago*, surveying the area, had been wrecked earlier, Magellan started south again. On October 21, 1520, he rounded the Cape of the Virgins (Cabo Vírgenes, Argentina) and at approximately 52°50' S entered the passage that proved to be the strait of his seeking, later to bear his name. The *San Antonio* having deserted, only three of his ships reached the western end of the passage. At the news that the ocean had been sighted, the iron-willed admiral reportedly broke down and cried with joy.

On November 28, 1520, the *Trinidad*, the *Concepción*, and the *Victoria* entered the "Sea of the South," from their calm crossing later called the Pacific Ocean. Tortured by thirst, stricken by scurvy, feeding on rat-fouled biscuits, and finally reduced to eating the leather off the yardarms, the crews, driven first by the Peru Current and throughout the voyage by the relentless determination of Magellan, made the great crossing of the Pacific. Until December 18 they had sailed near the Chilean coast; then Magellan took a course northwestward. Not until January 24, 1521, was land sighted, probably Pukapuka Atoll in the Tuamotu Archipelago (now part of French Polynesia). Crossing the equinoctial line at approximately 158° W on February 13, the voyagers on March 6 made first landfall at Guam in the Mariana Islands, where they obtained fresh food for the first time in 99 days.

A statement sent to King Charles by Magellan before he left Spain suggests that he knew (probably partly from Serrão's letters or perhaps from his own possible voyage there in 1511–12) the approximate position of the Moluccas. In sailing from the Marianas to the islands later called the Philippines, instead of heading directly to the Spice Islands, he was doubtless dominated by the idea of gathering provisions and the advantage of securing a base before visiting the Moluccas. Thus, leaving the Marianas on March 9, 1521, Magellan steered west-southwestward to the Philippines, where, in late March and early April, he secured the first alliance in the Pacific for Spain (at Limasawa Island) and the conversion to Christianity of the ruler of Cebu Island and his chief men. Weeks later, however, Magellan was killed in a fight with the people of nearby Mactan Island.

CIRCUMNAVIGATION OF THE GLOBE

After Magellan's death only two of the ships, the *Trinidad* and the *Victoria*, reached the Moluccas. Gonzalo Gómez de Espinosa, Magellan's master-at-arms, attempted to return to Spain on the *Trinidad*, but it soon became evident that the ship was no longer seaworthy. Espinosa himself then was arrested by Portuguese officials and imprisoned. Cano, originally master of the *Concepción* and a participant in the mutiny at Port Saint Julian, took the chance of continuing westward with the *Victoria*, as he likely determined that the crew would not survive another extremely hard voyage across the Pacific. On his way across the Indian Ocean and up the western coast of Africa, he had the good fortune of not being intercepted by the Portuguese ships that by then regularly traveled the route. For taking home to Spain, on September 8, 1522, the leaking but spice-laden *Victoria*, with only 17 other European survivors and a small number of Moluccans, "weaker than men have ever been before," Cano received from Emperor Charles an augmentation to his coat of arms—a globe with the inscription "Primus circumdedisti me" ("You were the first to encircle me").

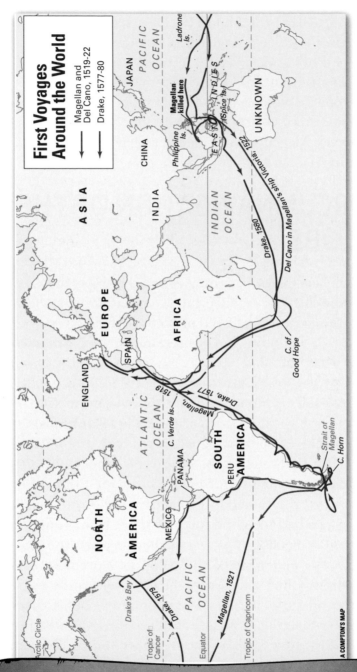

The voyages of Ferdinand Magellan (1519–22) and Francis Drake (1577–80), the first two circumnavigations of the world.

ASSESSMENT

Magellan was undoubtedly one of the most skilled sailors of the great age of European maritime discoveries. Yet because he sailed in the service of the king of Spain, Portuguese historians have tended not to grant him the credit given to other eminent Portuguese navigators, such as Bartolomeu Dias and Vasco da Gama. Spanish historians, on the other hand, have preferred to emphasize the role of the Spanish (actually Basque) navigator Cano. However, Magellan did only what his predecessors Christopher Columbus, John Cabot, and Amerigo Vespucci had done: lacking the opportunity to pursue their goals under the sponsorship of their own country, they looked for support elsewhere. This was a common attitude in the 15th and 16th centuries, a time before the age of nationalism and a time when men pledged allegiance not to the place where they were born but to a king. The early explorers served the monarch who supported their goals of fortune and fame, and the monarch in turn accepted the fealty of men who would enhance the wealth and power of the crown.

Notwithstanding the neglect of Iberian historians, Magellan's complex character, his uncommonly eventful life, and the extreme difficulty of the voyage itself have fueled imaginations ever since the first account of the expedition—recorded by one of its few survivors, Antonio Pigafetta—appeared in the 16th century. Later biographers, such as the 20th-century writer Stefan Zweig, have portrayed Magellan as a symbol of the human capacity to succeed against all odds. Other contemporary authors have attempted to illustrate the magnitude of his accomplishment by likening his voyage through unknown waters to the first explorations of space.

Map of South America and the surrounding Southern Ocean (Atlantic) and Great South Sea (Pacific), from the 1st edition of Encyclopædia Britannica, *published 1768–71.* Encyclopædia Britannica, Inc.

Such a comparison might even be said to underestimate Magellan's feat—a 16th-century maritime expedition was arguably much more unpredictable, and hence far more perilous, than computer-assisted space travel—but in any case, the achievements of Magellan were of profound importance. His supreme accomplishment was the discovery and crossing of the South American strait that bears his name—a major navigational task, considering the knowledge of the period. Moreover, being the first to traverse the "Sea of the South" from east to west, he demonstrated the immensity of the Pacific Ocean and the challenges it posed to navigation. Finally, the idea of the voyage itself had relied on the not-undisputed idea of a spherical Earth. The circumnavigation completed by Magellan's expedition thus confirmed the conception of the world as a globe.

PANFILO DE NARVÁEZ

(b. c. 1478, Valladolid, Castile [Spain]—d. November 1528, Gulf of Mexico)

Panfilo de Narváez was a Spanish conquistador, colonial official, and explorer who led an expedition along the northeastern and northern coasts of the Gulf of Mexico.

Narváez entered military service as a youth and arrived in Jamaica as one of the island's first settlers. Later, he commanded a company of archers during Diego Velásquez' campaign to conquer and pacify Cuba. He was rewarded for his services with public offices and extensive land grants on the island. In March 1520 he left Cuba, commanding a fleet of ships and about 900 men with orders from Velásquez to capture and replace Hernán Cortés as ruler of Mexico. Cortés, who had been charged with treason and disloyalty, defeated the expedition. Narváez was taken prisoner with most of his men; he was released the next year on orders from Spain and returned to Cuba.

In 1526 Narváez received authorization and numerous governing titles from King Charles I (the Holy Roman emperor Charles V) to subdue and colonize vast lands from Florida westward. He sailed from Spain on June 17, 1527, with five ships and about 600 soldiers, sailors, and colonists. In Santo Domingo, 140 men deserted the expedition, and in Cuba, a hurricane sank two of the ships, killing 50 men and several horses. Narváez remained in Cuba until late February 1528, then sailed with five ships and 400 followers to the region around Tampa Bay in Florida. After claiming the land for Spain, Narváez began an overland expedition in May with about 300 men. The force made a difficult and distressing march northward, continually fighting Indians, until the survivors reached the area of present-day St. Marks, Florida, near the end of July.

Since the vessels from the expedition failed to come to their aid, Narváez' suffering survivors had to construct additional ships. They built five vessels, and in late September, 245 men sailed along the coast, hoping to reach Mexico. The ships drifted along the northern part of the Gulf of Mexico, passing Pensacola Bay and the mouth of the Mississippi River. As the journey progressed, the boats were gradually lost, and at about the beginning of November 1528, Narváez disappeared when his own vessel was suddenly blown out to sea. Only four men survived the expedition.

PEDRO DE ALVARADO

(b. c. 1485, Badajoz, Castile [Spain]—d. 1541, in or near Guadalajara, New Spain [now in Mexico])

The Spanish conquistador and explorer Pedro de Alvarado was one of the conquerors of Mexico and Central America for Spain.

Alvarado went to Santo Domingo in 1510 and in 1518 commanded one of Juan de Grijalba's ships sent from Cuba to explore the Yucatán Peninsula. In February 1519 he accompanied the army, led from Cuba by Hernán Cortés, that was to conquer Mexico. Alvarado was first placed in charge of Tenochtitlán (later Mexico City) in 1520 when Cortés left the city to meet a rival Spanish force on the coast. When Aztecs gathered in the square to celebrate the festival of Toxcatl, Alvarado feared an uprising and ordered his men to strike first. About 200 Aztec chiefs were massacred by Alvarado's men, who were in turn besieged in their quarters by an angry mob. Upon his return, Cortés learned of the attack and uprising and quickly planned a nighttime retreat from Tenochtitlán. On the night of June 30, 1520, known as *noche triste* (sad night), Cortés and his men attempted to leave the city quietly but were spotted by the Aztecs. Fierce fighting erupted, and Alvarado, who was leading the rear guard, narrowly escaped, thanks largely to a spectacular leap across a canal. The Spanish recaptured Tenochtitlán in 1521, and in 1522 Alvarado became the city's first *alcalde* (mayor or principal magistrate).

In 1523 Alvarado conquered the Quiché and Cakchiquel of Guatemala and in 1524 founded Santiago de los Caballeros de Guatemala (Ciudad Vieja; present-day Antigua, Guatemala). This town became the first capital of the captaincy general of Guatemala, later including much of Central America, of which Alvarado was governor (1527–31).

In 1534 Alvarado led an unlicensed expedition to Quito (Ecuador), but in 1535 he sold his ships and munitions to Diego de Almagro, one of Francisco Pizarro's captains. He then returned to Guatemala and in 1537 to Spain, where he was confirmed as governor of Guatemala for seven years and was given a charter to explore Mexico. He arrived in Honduras in 1539 and died while attempting to quell an Indian uprising in central Mexico.

HERNÁN CORTÉS

(b. 1485, Medellín, near Mérida, Extremadura, Castile [Spain]—d. December 2, 1547, Castilleja de la Cuesta, near Sevilla)

The Spanish conquistador and explorer Hernán Cortés (or Cortéz) overthrew the Aztec empire (1519–21) and won Mexico for the crown of Spain.

Cortés was the son of Martín Cortés de Monroy and of Doña Catalina Pizarro Altamarino—names of ancient lineage. "They had little wealth, but much honour," according to Cortés' secretary, Francisco López de Gómara, who tells how, at age 14, the young Hernán was sent to study at Salamanca, in west-central Spain, "because he was very intelligent and clever in everything he did." Gómara went on to describe him as ruthless, haughty, mischievous, and quarrelsome, "a source of trouble to his parents." Certainly he was "much given to women," frustrated by provincial life, and excited by stories of the Indies Columbus had just discovered. He set out for the east coast port of Valencia with the idea of serving in the Italian wars, but instead he "wandered idly about for nearly a year." Clearly Spain's southern ports, with ships coming in full of the wealth

Hernán Cortés. Universal Images Group/Getty Images

and colour of the Indies, proved a greater attraction. He finally sailed for the island of Hispaniola (now Haiti and Dominican Republic, or Santo Domingo) in 1504.

YEARS IN HISPANIOLA AND CUBA

In Hispaniola he became a farmer and notary to a town council; for the first six years or so, he seems to have been content to establish his position. He contracted syphilis and, as a result, missed the ill-fated expeditions of Diego de Nicuesa and Alonso de Ojeda, which sailed for the South American mainland in 1509. By 1511 he had recovered, and he sailed with Diego Velázquez to conquer Cuba. There Velázquez was appointed governor, and Cortés clerk to the treasurer. Cortés received a *repartimiento* (gift of land and Indian slaves) and the first house in the new capital of Santiago. He was now in a position of some power and the man to whom dissident elements in the colony began to turn for leadership.

Cortés was twice elected *alcalde* (mayor) of the town of Santiago and was a man who "in all he did, in his presence, bearing, conversation, manner of eating and of dressing, gave signs of being a great lord." It was therefore to Cortés that Velázquez turned when, after news had come of the progress of Juan de Grijalba's efforts to establish a colony on the mainland, it was decided to send him help. An agreement appointing Cortés captain general of a new expedition was signed in October 1518. Experience of the rough-and-tumble of New World politics advised Cortés to move fast, before Velázquez changed his mind. His sense of the dramatic, his long experience as an administrator, the knowledge gained from so many failed expeditions, above all his ability as a speaker gathered to him six ships and 300 men, all in less than a month. The reaction of Velázquez was predictable; his jealousy aroused, he resolved to place leadership of the expedition in other hands. Cortés, however, put hastily to sea to raise more men and ships in other Cuban ports.

THE EXPEDITION TO MEXICO

When Cortés finally sailed for the coast of Yucatán on February 18, 1519, he had 11 ships, 508 soldiers, about 100 sailors, and—most important—16 horses. In March 1519 he landed at Tabasco, where he stayed for a time in order to gain intelligence from the local Indians. He won them over and received presents from them, including 20 women, one of whom, Marina ("Malinche"), became his mistress and interpreter and bore him a son, Martín. Cortés sailed to another spot on the southeastern Mexican coast and founded Veracruz, mainly to have himself elected captain general and chief justice by his soldiers as citizens, thus shaking off the authority of Velázquez. On the mainland Cortés did what no other expedition leader had done: he exercised and disciplined his army, welding it into a cohesive force. But the ultimate expression of his determination to deal with disaffection occurred when he sank his ships. By that single action he committed himself and his entire force to survival by conquest.

Cortés then set out for the Mexican interior, relying sometimes on force, sometimes on amity toward the local Indian peoples, but always careful to keep conflict with them to a strict minimum. The key to Cortés' subsequent conquests lay in the political crisis within the Aztec empire; the Aztecs were bitterly resented by many of the subject peoples who had to pay tribute to them. The ability of Cortés as a leader is nowhere more apparent than in his quick grasp of the situation—a grasp that was ultimately to give him more than 200,000 Indian allies. The nation of Tlaxcala, for instance, which was in a state of chronic war with Montezuma II, ruler of the Aztec empire of Mexico, resisted Cortés at first but became his most faithful ally. Rejecting all of Montezuma's threats and blandishments to keep him away from Tenochtitlán or Mexico, the capital (rebuilt as Mexico City after 1521), Cortés entered the city on November 8, 1519, with his small Spanish force and only 1,000 Tlaxcaltecs. In accordance with the diplomatic customs of Mexico, Montezuma received him with great honour. Cortés soon decided to seize Montezuma in order to hold the country through its monarch and achieve not only its political conquest but its religious conversion.

Spanish politics and envy were to bedevil Cortés throughout his meteoric career. Cortés soon heard of the arrival of a Spanish force from Cuba, led by Pánfilo Narváez, to deprive Cortés of his command at a time (mid-1520) when he was holding the Aztec capital of Tenochtitlán by little more than the force of his personality. Leaving a garrison in Tenochtitlán of 80 Spaniards and a few hundred Tlaxcaltecs commanded by his most reckless captain, Pedro de Alvarado, Cortés marched against Narváez, defeated him, and enlisted his army in his own forces. On his return, he found the Spanish garrison in Tenochtitlán besieged by the Aztecs after Alvarado had massacred many leading Aztec chiefs during a festival. Hard pressed and lacking food, Cortés decided to leave the city by night. The Spaniards' retreat from the capital was performed, but with a heavy loss in lives and most of the treasure they had accumulated. After six days of retreat Cortés won the battle of Otumba over the Aztecs sent in pursuit (July 7, 1520).

Cortés eventually rejoined his Tlaxcalan allies and reorganized his forces before again marching on Tenochtitlán in December 1520. After subduing the

Cortés (left) *meeting with Montezuma, ruler of the Aztec empire.* Universal Images Group/Getty Images

neighbouring territories he laid siege to the city itself, conquering it street by street until its capture was completed on August 13, 1521. This victory marked the fall of the Aztec empire. Cortés had become the absolute ruler of a huge territory extending from the Caribbean Sea to the Pacific Ocean.

In the meantime, Velázquez was mounting an insidious political attack on Cortés in Spain through Bishop Juan Rodríguez de Fonseca and the Council of the Indies. Fully conscious of the vulnerability of a successful conqueror whose field of operations was 5,000 miles (8,000 km) from the centre of political power, Cortés countered with lengthy and detailed dispatches—five remarkable letters to the Spanish king Charles I (Holy Roman emperor Charles V). His acceptance by the Indians and even his popularity as a relatively benign ruler was such that he could have established Mexico as an independent kingdom. Indeed, this is what the Council of the Indies feared. But his upbringing in a feudal world in which the king commanded absolute allegiance was against it.

LATER YEARS

In 1524 his restless urge to explore and conquer took him south to the jungles of Honduras. The two arduous years he spent on this disastrous expedition damaged his health and his position. His property was seized by the officials he had left in charge, and reports of the cruelty of their administration and the chaos it created aroused concern in Spain. Cortés' fifth letter to the Spanish king attempts to justify his reckless behaviour and concludes with a bitter attack on "various and powerful rivals and enemies" who have "obscured the eyes of your Majesty." But it was his misfortune that he was not dealing simply with a king of Spain but with an emperor who ruled most of Europe and who had little time for distant colonies, except insofar as they contributed to his treasury. The Spanish bureaucrats sent out a commission of inquiry under Luis Ponce de León, and, when he died almost immediately, Cortés was accused of poisoning him and was forced to retire to his estate.

In 1528 Cortés sailed for Spain to plead his cause in person with the king. He brought with him a great wealth of treasure and a magnificent entourage. He was received by Charles at his court at Toledo, confirmed as captain general (but not as governor), and created marqués del Valle de Oaxaca. He also remarried, into a ducal family. He returned to New Spain in 1530 to find the country in a state of anarchy and so many accusations made against him—even that he had murdered his first wife, Catalina, who had died that year—that, after reasserting his position and reestablishing some sort of order, he retired to his estates at Cuernavaca, about 30 miles (48 km) south of Mexico City. There he concentrated on the building of his palace and on Pacific exploration.

Finally a viceroy was appointed, after which, in 1540, Cortés returned to Spain. By then he had become thoroughly disillusioned, his life made miserable by litigation. All the rest is anticlimax. "I am old, poor and in debt... again and again I have begged your Majesty...." In the end he was permitted to return to Mexico, but he died before he had even reached Sevilla (Seville).

GIOVANNI DA VERRAZZANO

(b. 1485, Tuscany [Italy]—d. 1528, Lesser Antilles)

The Italian navigator Giovanni da Verrazzano (or Verrazano) was an explorer for France and became the first European to sight New York and Narragansett bays.

After his education in Florence, Verrazzano moved to Dieppe, France, and entered that nation's maritime service. He made several voyages to the Levant, and in 1523 he secured two ships for a voyage backed by the French king to discover a westward passage to Asia. In January 1524 he sailed one of those vessels, *La Dauphine*, to the New World and reached

Giovanni da Verrazzano. Encyclopædia Britannica, Inc.

Cape Fear about the beginning of March. Verrazzano then sailed northward, exploring the eastern coast of North America. He made several discoveries on the voyage, including the sites of present-day New York Harbor, Block Island, and Narragansett Bay, and was the first European explorer to name newly discovered North American sites after persons and places in the Old World.

Verrazzano wrote interesting, though sometimes inaccurate, accounts of the lands and inhabitants that he encountered. His explorations concluded at the eastern part of Newfoundland. His return to France on July 8, 1524, gave King Francis I his nation's claim to the New World.

Verrazzano undertook two more voyages to the Americas. In 1527 he commanded a fleet of ships on an expedition to Brazil that returned profitable dyewood to France. His final voyage began in the spring of 1528, when he sailed with his brother, Girolamo, from Dieppe with two or three ships. The fleet sailed to Florida, the Bahamas, and finally the Lesser Antilles. He anchored there off one of the islands (apparently Guadeloupe), went ashore, and was captured, killed, and eaten by cannibals.

JUAN DE GRIJALBA

(b. 1480?, Cuéllar, Spain—d. January 21, 1527, Honduras)

The Spanish explorer Juan de Grijalba (or Grijalva) was a nephew of the conquistador Diego Velázquez. He was one of the first to explore the eastern coast of Mexico.

Grijalba accompanied Velázquez in the conquest of Cuba (1511) and founded the city of Trinidad (1514). In 1518, Velázquez, as governor of Cuba, sent Grijalba to explore the Yucatán Peninsula. Setting sail from Cuba with four ships and about 200 men, Grijalba became the first navigator to set foot on Mexican soil and the first to use the term *New Spain*. He and his men mapped rivers and discovered Cozumel Island. During their explorations, the men heard tales of a rich civilization in the interior. At last Grijalba met with its representatives, thus becoming the first European to learn of the existence of the Aztec empire farther to the north.

When he returned to Cuba, his uncle was furious that his nephew had made no attempt at settlement, although Grijalba's orders had been to explore only. As a result, Grijalba was passed over and the job of colonization was given to Hernán Cortés. Grijalba accompanied Cortés on his expedition (1519), but it was Grijalba's explorations that paved the way for Cortés, thereby leading to the conquest of Mexico.

ÁLVAR NÚÑEZ CABEZA DE VACA

(b. c. 1490, Extremadura, Castile [now in Spain]—d. c. 1560, Sevilla, Spain)

Álvares Núñez Cabeza de Vaca was a Spanish explorer who spent eight years in the Gulf of Mexico region of present-day Texas.

Núñez was treasurer to the Spanish expedition under Pánfilo de Narváez that reached what is now Tampa Bay, Florida, in 1528.

By September all but his party of 60 had perished; it reached the shore near present-day Galveston, Texas. Of this group only 15 were still alive the following spring, and eventually only Núñez and three others remained. In the following years he and his companions spent much time among nomadic Indians, serving as slaves in order to be cared for by them. Núñez later reported that he had pretended at times to be a healer in order to receive better treatment and more food from the Indians. Though he found only the gravest hardship and poverty during his wanderings, he made his way back to Mexico in 1536. He recounted his adventures in *Naufragios* ... (1542; "Shipwrecks ..."). He was later appointed governor of the province of Río de la Plata in South America, and from November 1541 to March 1542 he blazed a route from Santos, Brazil, to Asunción, Paraguay. His power was usurped by a rebel governor, Domingo Martinez de Irala, who imprisoned him and had him deported to Spain (1545), where he was convicted of malfeasance in office and banished to service in Africa. His *La relación y comentarios* ... (1555), describing his journey from Santos to Asunción, is a valuable geographic work.

FRANCISCO DE ORELLANA

(b. c. 1490, Trujillo, Extremadura, Castile
[Spain]—d. c. 1546, Amazon River)

The Spanish soldier and conquistador Francisco de Orellana was the first European explorer of the Amazon River basin.

After participating with Francisco Pizarro in the conquest of Peru in 1535, Orellana moved to Guayaquil and was named governor of that area in 1538. When Pizarro's half brother, Gonzalo, prepared an expedition to explore the regions east of Quito, Orellana was appointed his lieutenant. In April 1541 he was sent ahead of the main party to seek provisions, taking a brigantine with 50 soldiers. He reached the junction of the Napo and Marañón rivers, where his group persuaded him of the impossibility of returning to Pizarro. Instead, he entered upon an exploration of the Amazon system. Drifting with the current, he reached the mouth of the river in August 1542. Proceeding to Trinidad, he finally returned to Spain, where he told of hoards of gold and cinnamon and of encounters with tribes led by women resembling the Amazons of Greek mythology—a comparison that is presumed to have led him to name the river the Amazon.

Orellana sought the right to explore and exploit the lands that he had discovered. Because the Spanish crown was involved in controversy with Portugal over the ownership of the area, it could provide him with only some assistance but no official support. His return to the Amazon proved a disaster. Ships and men were lost on the passage to America, and Orellana's vessel capsized near the mouth of the great river and he drowned.

JACQUES CARTIER

(b. 1491, Saint-Malo, Brittany, France—d. September 1, 1557, near Saint-Malo)

The French mariner Jacques Cartier led the explorations of the Canadian coast and the St. Lawrence

River (1534, 1535, 1541–42) that laid the basis for later French claims to North America. Cartier also is credited with naming Canada, though he used the name—derived from the Huron-Iroquois *kanata*, meaning a village or settlement—to refer only to the area around what is now Quebec city.

Jacques Cartier. Stock Montage/Archive Photos/Getty Images

Cartier appears to have voyaged to the Americas, particularly Brazil, prior to his three major North American voyages. When King Francis I of France decided in 1534 to send an expedition to explore the northern lands in the hope of discovering gold, spices, and a passage to Asia, Cartier received the commission. He sailed from Saint-Malo on April 20, 1534, with two ships and 61 men. Reaching North America a few weeks later, Cartier traveled along the west coast of Newfoundland, discovered Prince Edward Island, and explored the Gulf of St. Lawrence as far as Anticosti Island. Having seized two Indians at the Gaspé Peninsula, he sailed back to France.

His report piqued the curiosity of Francis I sufficiently for him to send Cartier back the following year, with three ships and 110 men, to explore further. Guided by the two Indians he had brought back, he sailed up the St. Lawrence as far as Quebec and established a base near an Iroquois village. In September he proceeded with a small party as far as the island of Montreal, where navigation was barred by rapids. He was warmly welcomed by the resident Iroquois, but he spent only a few hours among them before returning to winter at his base. He had, however, learned from the Indians that two rivers led farther west to lands where gold, silver, copper, and spices abounded.

The severity of the winter came as a terrible shock; no Europeans since the Vikings had wintered that far north on the American continent, and a mild winter was expected because Quebec lay at a lower latitude than Paris. Scurvy claimed 25 of Cartier's men. To make matters worse, the explorers earned the enmity of the Iroquois. Thus, in May, as soon as the river was free of ice, they treacherously seized some of the Iroquois chiefs and sailed for France. Cartier was able to report only that great riches lay farther in the interior and that a great river, said to be 800 leagues (about 2,000 miles [3,200 km]) long, possibly led to Asia.

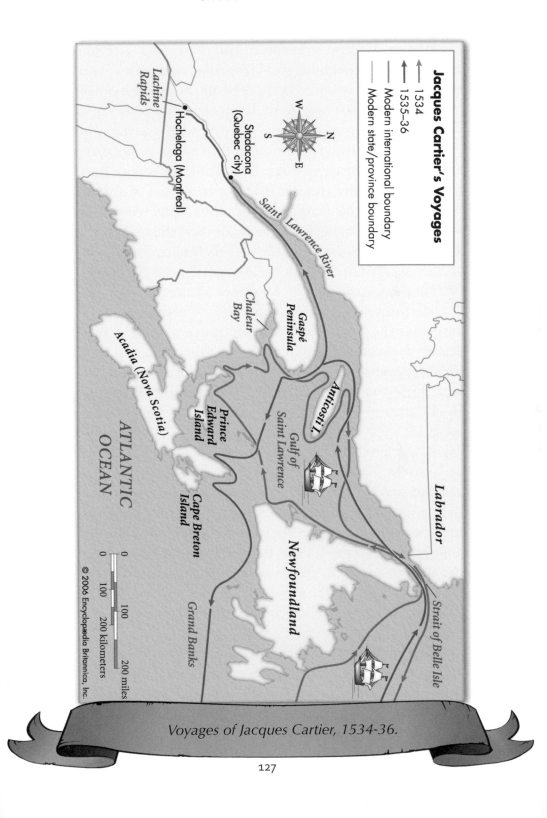

Jacques Cartier's Voyages

↑ 1534
↑ 1535–36
— Modern international boundary
— Modern state/province boundary

Lachine Rapids

Hochelaga (Montreal)

Stadacona (Quebec city)

Saint Lawrence River

Chaleur Bay

Gaspé Peninsula

Acadia (Nova Scotia)

Prince Edward Island

Anticosti I.

Gulf of Saint Lawrence

Labrador

Cape Breton Island

ATLANTIC OCEAN

Newfoundland

Strait of Belle Isle

Grand Banks

© 2006 Encyclopædia Britannica, Inc.

0   100   200 kilometers
0   100   200 miles

Voyages of Jacques Cartier, 1534-36.

War in Europe prevented Francis I from sending another expedition until 1541. This time, to secure French title against the counterclaims of Spain, he commissioned a nobleman, Jean-François de La Rocque de Roberval, to establish a colony in the lands discovered by Cartier, who was appointed Roberval's subaltern. Cartier sailed first, arriving at Quebec on August 23; Roberval was delayed until the following year. Cartier again visited Montreal, but as before he remained only a few hours and failed to go even the few miles necessary to get beyond the rapids. The subsequent maps based on the knowledge he provided fail to indicate that he had reached a large island at the confluence of the Ottawa and St. Lawrence rivers.

The winter at his new base above Quebec proved as severe as the earlier one. Cartier appears to have been unable to maintain discipline among his men, and their actions again aroused the hostility of the local Indians. But what were thought to be gold and diamonds were found in abundance. In the spring, not waiting for Roberval to arrive with the main body of colonists, Cartier abandoned the base and sailed for France. En route he stopped at Newfoundland, where he encountered Roberval, who ordered him back to Quebec. Cartier, however, stole away during the night and continued back to France. There, his mineral specimens were found to be valueless. Roberval enjoyed no better success. After one winter he abandoned the plan to found a colony and returned to France. The disappointment at these meagre results was very great. France did not again show interest in these new lands for more than half a century.

Cartier received no new commissions from the crown. He apparently spent his remaining years attending to his business affairs at his estate near Saint-Malo. His claim to fame rests on his exploration of the St. Lawrence River to the height of navigation. Yet his failure to proceed any farther (when it would have been easy to do so), his treacherous dealings with the Iroquois, and his leaving Roberval in the lurch detract somewhat from his stature.

SEBASTIÁN DE BENALCÁZAR

(b. c. 1495, Benalcázar, Spain—d. 1551,
Cartagena, New Granada [now in Colombia])

Sebastián de Benalcázar (Belalcázar, or Belaicázar) was the Spanish conqueror of Nicaragua, Ecuador, and southwestern Colombia. He captured Quito and founded the cities of Guayaquil in Ecuador and Popayán in Colombia.

Going to the New World in 1519, Benalcázar (also known as Sebastián Moyano) became an officer in the forces of Pedro Arias Dávila and in 1524 conquered Nicaragua. Joining Francisco Pizarro's expedition to Peru in 1531, he was given command of the supporting base at Piura. In 1533 he set out to conquer what is now Ecuador. Defeating the Inca chief Rumiñahui, Benalcázar occupied the Indian city of Quito on December 6, 1534. In 1535 he founded a settlement that was later moved to a more healthful site and developed into the modern Guayaquil. Benalcázar led an expedition in search of the mythical Eldorado, believed to be a region abounding in gold. He entered the Popayán region of Colombia, founded the city of Popayán in 1537, and became governor of the district.

The close of Benalcázar's life was embittered by disputes with other Spanish leaders. He died while under indictment for the killing of one of them, Jorge Robledo.

GONZALO JIMÉNEZ DE QUESADA

(b. c. 1495, Córdoba or Granada, Spain—d.
February 16, 1579, Mariquita, New Granada
[now in Colombia])

The Spanish government official and conquistador Gonzalo Jiménez de Quesada led the expedition that won the region of New Granada (Colombia) for Spain.

Trained as a lawyer in Granada, Quesada sailed to the New World in 1535 to serve as the chief magistrate for the colony of Santa Marta, on the northern coast of South America. The following year, although he had no military experience, Quesada led an expedition of 900 men up the Magdalena River into the interior of New Granada. After eight months of marching through tropical forests and struggling with hostile Indians, the expedition succeeded in penetrating the great central plain of Colombia—the land of the Chibcha Indians, a group of tribes that had established a more centralized political state than in other nearby peoples. The ruler of the Chibchas, the Zipa of Bogotá, fled as Quesada's army approached, and the conquest appeared to have been accomplished. Toward the end of 1538, however, two rival conquistadores—Sebastián de Belalcázar from Quito and Nikolaus Federmann from Venezuela—challenged Quesada's claim to the New Granada triumph. The three rivals agreed to submit their case to Madrid. In July 1539 Quesada sailed from Cartagena to Spain to plead before the crown his right of conquest, but he succeeded only in winning for himself an honorary title.

On his return to New Granada, he became at once the most influential person in the colony, protecting the colonists from the severity of officials and restraining the rapacity of the *comenderos* (large landholders). Yet his own thirst for conquest (and for gold) was not yet quenched. In 1569 he set out with 500 men to search for the mythical Eldorado but returned after two years' wanderings with only 25 of his original company. The least contentious of the great conquistadores, he retired to La Suesca, his country house in New Granada, where he wrote a book about his campaigns, which has been lost. He died of leprosy.

MARCOS DE NIZA

(b. c. 1495, Nice, Savoy [now in France]—d. March 25, 1558, Mexico)

Marcos de Niza (also called Fray Marcos) was a Franciscan friar and an explorer who claimed to have sighted the legendary "Seven Golden Cities of Cibola" in what is now western New Mexico.

Niza went to the Americas in 1531 and served in Peru, Guatemala, and Mexico. At Culiacán, Mexico, he freed Indian slaves from regions to the north. Under orders from the viceroy Antonio de Mendoza, Niza and a Moor, Estéban (Estevanico), led an expedition across the desert to the cities of Cibola (1539). Estéban was killed, but Niza claimed to have come within sight of large towns rich in precious stones, gold, and silver. The exaggerated promise of wealth stimulated interest in the further exploration of northern New Spain, but the following year soldiers with the Francisco de Coronado expedition found the "seven cities" to be small and poor Indian pueblos. Niza became provincial of his order for Mexico in 1541.

HERNANDO DE SOTO

(b. c. 1496/97, Jerez de los Caballeros, Badajoz, Spain—d. May 21, 1542, along the Mississippi River [in present-day Louisiana, U.S.])

The Spanish explorer and conquistador Hernando (or Fernando) de Soto participated in the conquests of Central America and Peru and, in the course of exploring what was to become the southeastern United States, discovered the Mississippi River.

EARLY YEARS

De Soto spent his youth in the family manor house at Jerez de los Caballeros. His parents intended him to be a lawyer, but in 1514, while still in his teens, he told his father of his desire to go to the Indies, and he left for Sevilla (Seville). Despite his youth, de Soto's zeal and his prowess as a horseman helped gain him a place on the 1514 expedition of Pedro Arias Dávila to the West Indies. In Panama, de Soto quickly made his mark as a trader and expeditioner, reaping high profits by his skill and daring. By 1520 he had

Hernando de Soto, engraving. Encyclopædia Britannica, Inc.

accumulated considerable capital through his slave trading in Nicaragua and on the Isthmus of Panama, after successful partnerships with Hernán Ponce de León and Francisco Campañón. In 1524–27 de Soto defeated his archrival, Gil González de Ávila, in a struggle for control of Nicaragua, and he subsequently expanded his trade in Indian slaves.

In 1530 de Soto lent Francisco Pizarro two ships to investigate reports of gold located south of Darién on the Pacific coast (now in northwestern Colombia). After de Soto's patron, Dávila, died in 1531 and Pizarro's expedition confirmed the reports of gold, de Soto joined the new enterprise. In return for the use of his ships, Pizarro named de Soto his chief lieutenant, and the conquest of Peru began the next year (1532). De Soto, as the expedition's captain of horse, was the driving force in the Spaniards' defeat of the Incas at Cajamarca, and he was the first European to make contact with the Inca emperor Atahuallpa.

Following the Spaniards' capture of Atahuallpa, de Soto seized Cuzco, the Inca capital. For political reasons, he became the emperor's friend and protector, but Pizarro, fearing Atahuallpa's influence over his Inca subjects, had the emperor executed even though the latter's subjects had raised an enormous ransom in gold in order to ensure his release. Dissatisfied with Pizarro's leadership and coveting a governorship of his own, de Soto returned to Spain in 1536. The shares that he had accumulated in the sack of Peru, though less than half of Pizarro's, made him one of the wealthiest of the returning conquistadors.

In Spain de Soto married Isabel de Bobadillo, daughter of Dávila, and was accepted into the prestigious Order of Santiago. He grew restless in Spain, however, and in 1537 he sought special permission to conquer Ecuador, with special rights to the Amazon River basin. Instead, he was commissioned by the Spanish crown to conquer what is now Florida. In addition, he was made governor of Cuba.

EXPLORATION OF SOUTHERN NORTH AMERICA

In April 1538 de Soto embarked from the port of Sanlúcar de Barrameda in command of 10 ships and 700 men. After

Hernando de Soto (centre) landing on the coast of Florida.
ClassicStock.com/SuperStock

a brief stop in Cuba, the expedition landed in May 1539 on the coast of Florida, at a point somewhere between present-day Tampa Bay and Charlotte Harbor. After spending the winter farther north in Florida at the small Indian village of Apalache (near present-day Tallahassee), de Soto moved farther northward into and through what is now Georgia and then westward through the present-day territory of the Carolinas and Tennessee, led by native guides whom he abducted along the way. Though he did not find the gold he was looking for, he did collect a valuable assortment of pearls at a place called Cofitachequi, in present-day Georgia or South Carolina (sources differ on its location). Near Lookout Mountain in southeastern Tennessee, de Soto and his men turned southward into Alabama and headed toward Mobile Bay, where they expected to rendezvous with their ships. But at the fortified Indian town of Mauvila (near Mobile), a confederation of Indians attacked the Spaniards in October 1540. The natives were decimated, but the Spanish were also severely crippled, losing most of their equipment and all their pearls.

After a month's rest, de Soto decided to turn north once again and head inland in search of treasure. This was a fateful decision that was to have disastrous results. Moving northwest through Alabama and then west through Mississippi, de Soto's party was attacked relentlessly by Indians. On May 21, 1541, the Spaniards saw for the first time the Mississippi River, the "Father of the Water" south of Memphis, Tennessee. They crossed the river and made their way through Arkansas and Louisiana. Then, early in 1542, de Soto turned back to the Mississippi River. Overcome by fever, he died in Louisiana, and his comrades buried his body in the Mississippi. Luis de Moscoso, whom de Soto had named his successor, led the expedition's remnants (half the original party) down the Mississippi on rafts, and they reached Mexico in 1543.

DAVID REUBENI

(d. after 1532)

David Reubeni was a Jewish adventurer whose grandiose plans inspired the messianic visions of the martyr Solomon Molcho (died 1532). He claimed to be a prince descended from the tribe of Reuben (hence his name) of a Jewish state in Arabia. Reubeni gained the favour and protection of Pope Clement VII and King John III of Portugal with his forcefully stated plan to lead a Jewish army against the Turks in Palestine.

Under the influence of Reubeni's charismatic personality, a young Portuguese Marrano (a Jew forced to espouse Christianity), Solomon Molcho, openly adopted Judaism; his subsequent sermons inflamed the smoldering messianic hopes of many Jews. Reubeni rebuffed Molcho for his rashness; in turn, Reubeni aroused the displeasure of King John and was forced to leave Portugal.

Reubeni eventually went to Italy, only to find that Solomon Molcho had preceded him and was gaining a high reputation as an eloquent preacher of messianic visions. Joining forces, they left for Ratisbon (now Regensburg, Germany), to see the Holy Roman emperor Charles V, who had convened Parliament there. The two visionaries tried to persuade Charles to arm the Jews to fight the Turks; instead, they were imprisoned, fettered, and sent to Mantua, Italy, to face the Inquisition. Molcho was burned at the stake, while Reubeni was sent to a Spanish prison, where he died a few years later, probably by poisoning.

JEAN-FRANÇOIS DE LA ROCQUE DE ROBERVAL

(b. c. 1500, Carcassonne, France—d. 1560/61,
Paris)

French colonizer Jean-François de La Rocque, *sieur* (lord) de Roberval, was chosen by Francis I to create a settlement on North American lands found earlier by Jacques Cartier. Roberval was born into a noble family and lived at the court of Francis of Angoulême. Roberval converted to Protestantism and was outlawed, but he was able to return to France and resume living in the court of Francis, now King Francis I. He dissipated his fortune and borrowed from his relatives; he was ill-financed when Francis chose him in 1541 to be lieutenant general of the North American territory. He received a royal subsidy of 45,000 livres but needed considerably more, which he acquired as a pirate by seizing a number of English ships.

Roberval sailed for the New World in 1542 in command of the ships *Valentine*, *Anne*, and *Lèchefraye* with a band of French gentlemen and some convicts to do heavy labour. His mission was to colonize and convert the natives to Roman Catholicism (though he was a Protestant). Cartier was to have been his guide, but the impatient explorer had left the previous year. The two did meet in Newfoundland on June 8, but thereupon Cartier returned to France.

Roberval's company navigated the Gulf of St. Lawrence and then settled temporarily at Cartier's former headquarters at Cap Rouge (near present-day Quebec city). Roberval did some exploring in the area and suffered through a harsh winter with the company. He was a stern disciplinarian, although his pardon of a member of the crew who had killed one of the sailors is the oldest extant Canadian document, dated September 9, 1542. The settlement was short-lived, breaking up in 1543 and returning to France. Mineral wealth that he brought back turned out to be fool's gold and mica. Roberval was in ruins financially, and he barely managed to keep his estate at Roberval. According to tradition, he was attacked and killed when he and a group of coreligionists were emerging from a nighttime Calvinist meeting in Paris.

MARINA

(b. c. 1501, Painalla, Mexico—d. 1550, Spain)

The Mexican Indian princess Marina (also known as Malinche or Doña Marina) was one of a group of female slaves given as a peace offering to the Spanish conquistadors by the Tabascan Indians in 1519. She became mistress, guide, and interpreter to Hernán Cortés during his conquest of Mexico, and the success of his ventures was often directly attributable to her services.

Renouncing her Indian name, Malintzin, on her conversion to Christianity, Doña Marina served her adopted countrymen with dedication. Her intelligence, tact, and knowledge of the Maya language of the coast and the Nahuatl language of the interior extricated the Spaniards

Xaltelolco.

Doña Marina stands beside a seated Hernán Cortés in an illustration from Diego Muñoz Camargo's History of Tlaxcala. Universal Images Group/Getty Images

from many perilous situations. She bore Cortés a son, Martín, and later married one of his soldiers, Juan de Jaramillo, with whom she journeyed to Spain, where she was warmly received at the Spanish court.

GONZALO PIZARRO

(b. 1502?, Trujillo, Spain—d. April 10, 1548,
Cuzco, Peru)

G onzalo Pizarro was a Spanish conquistador and explorer and was the leader of antiroyal forces in Peru. He is considered by some historians to be the leader of the first genuine struggle by colonists for independence from Spanish domination in America.

A half brother of Francisco Pizarro, with whom he fought during the conquest of Peru (1531–33), Gonzalo received for his services extensive land grants and was made governor of Quito in 1539. In 1541, with 200 Spaniards, some 4,000 Indians, and numerous horses and other animals, he led an expedition into the unexplored region east of Quito. After his lieutenant, Francisco de Orellana, left him in search of provisions, Pizarro and his men waited in vain for his return. Forced to eat their dogs and horses, they finally staggered back to Quito in August 1542. Only a few Spaniards and no Indians survived the disastrous expedition.

On his return, Pizarro learned that his half brother Francisco had been assassinated in 1541 and that he had been ordered to dismiss his men. The king of Spain had promulgated new laws restricting the privileges of the conquistadores and protecting the rights of the Indians. Objecting to these edicts, the Spaniards intended to fight for their prerogatives and acclaimed Pizarro as the governor of Peru. As the leader of the antiroyal forces, he took the field against the viceroy Blasco Núñez Vela, winning the Battle of Anaquito in 1546, and against the viceroy Pedro de la Gasca in 1548. Defeated and captured by de la Gasca on April 9 of that year, Pizarro was executed the following day.

SAINT FRANCIS XAVIER

(b. April 7, 1506, Xavier Castle, near Sangüesa, Navarre [Spain]—d. December 3, 1552, Sancian [Shangchuan] Island, China; canonized March 12, 1622; feast day December 3)

Saint Francis Xavier (Spanish: San Francisco Javier, or Xavier) was the greatest Roman Catholic missionary of modern times and was instrumental in the establishment of Christianity in India, the Malay Archipelago, and Japan. In Paris in 1534 he pronounced vows as one of the first seven members of the Society of Jesus, or Jesuits, under the leadership of Ignatius of Loyola.

EARLY LIFE AND EDUCATION

Francis was born in Navarre (now in northern Spain), at the family castle of Xavier, where Basque was the native language. He was the third son of the president of the council of the king of Navarre, most of whose kingdom was soon to fall to the crown of Castile (1512). Francis grew

A statue of St. Francis Xavier in Melaka, Malaysia.
© Hoberman Collection/SuperStock

up at Xavier and received his early education there. As was often the case with younger sons of the nobility, he was destined for an ecclesiastical career, and in 1525 he journeyed to the University of Paris, the theological centre of Europe, to begin his studies.

In 1529, Ignatius Loyola, another Basque student, was assigned to room with Francis. A former soldier 15 years Xavier's senior, he had undergone a profound religious conversion and was then gathering about himself a group of men who shared his ideals. Gradually, Ignatius won over the initially recalcitrant Xavier, and Francis was among the band of seven who, in a chapel on Montmartre in Paris, on August 15, 1534, vowed lives of poverty and celibacy in imitation of Christ and solemnly promised to undertake a pilgrimage to the Holy Land and subsequently to devote themselves to the salvation of believers and unbelievers alike. Xavier then performed the Spiritual Exercises, a series of meditations lasting about 30 days and devised by Ignatius in light of his own experience of conversion to guide the individual toward greater generosity in the service of God and humanity. They implanted in Francis the motivation that carried him for the rest of his life and prepared the way for his recurrent mystical experiences.

MISSION TO INDIA

After all the members of the band had completed their studies, they reassembled in Venice, where Xavier was ordained priest on June 24, 1537. Having for more than a year sought passage to the Holy Land in vain, the seven, along with fresh recruits, went to Rome to put themselves at the disposal of the pope. Meanwhile, as a result of their preaching and care of the sick throughout central Italy, they had become so popular that many Catholic princes sought their services. One of these was King John III of Portugal, who desired diligent priests to minister to the Christians and to evangelize the peoples in his new Asian dominions. When illness prevented one of the two originally chosen for the task from departing, Ignatius designated Xavier as his substitute. The next day, March 15, 1540, Francis left Rome for South Asia, traveling first to Lisbon. In the following fall, Pope Paul III formally recognized the followers of Ignatius as a religious order, the Society of Jesus.

Francis disembarked in Goa, the centre of Portuguese activity in the East, on May 6, 1542; his companion had remained behind to work in Lisbon. Much of the next three years he spent on the southeastern coast of India among the poor pearl fishers, the Paravas. About 20,000 of them had accepted Baptism seven years before, chiefly to secure Portuguese support against their enemies; since then, however, they had been neglected. Using a small catechism he had translated into the native Tamil with the help of interpreters, Francis traveled tirelessly from village to village instructing and confirming them in their faith. His evident goodness and the force of his conviction overcame difficulties of verbal communication. Shortly afterward the Macuan people on the southwestern coast indicated their desire for Baptism, and, after brief instructions, in the last months of 1544 Xavier baptized 10,000 of them. He anticipated that the schools he planned and Portuguese pressure would keep them constant.

In the fall of 1545, news of opportunities for Christianity attracted him to the Malay Archipelago. Following several months of evangelization among the mixed population of the Portuguese commercial centre at Malacca (now Melaka, Malaysia), he moved on to found missions among the Malays and the headhunters in the Spice Islands (Moluccas). In 1548 he returned to India, where more Jesuits had since arrived to join him. In Goa the College of Holy Faith, founded several years previously, was turned over to the Jesuits, and Francis began to develop it into a centre for the education of native priests and catechists for the diocese of Goa, which stretched from the Cape of Good Hope, at the southern tip of Africa, to China.

YEARS IN JAPAN

Xavier's eyes, however, were now fixed on a land reached only five years before by Europeans: Japan. His conversations in Malacca with Anjiro, a Japanese man deeply interested in Christianity, had convinced him that the Japanese were culturally more sophisticated than the fishermen he had known in India or the headhunters of the Moluccas. On August 15, 1549, a Portuguese ship bearing Francis, the newly baptized Anjiro, and several companions entered the Japanese port of Kagoshima in southern Kyushu. Xavier's first letter from Japan, which was to be printed more than 30 times before the end of the century, revealed his enthusiasm for the Japanese, "the best people yet discovered." He grew conscious of the need to adapt his methods. His poverty that had so won the Paravas and Malays often repelled the Japanese, so he abandoned it for studied display when this was called for. In late 1551, having received no mail since his arrival in Japan, Francis decided to return temporarily to India, leaving to the care of his companions about 2,000 Christians in five communities.

Back in India, administrative affairs awaited him as the superior of the newly erected Jesuit Province of the Indies. Meanwhile, he had come to realize that the way to the conversion of Japan lay through China; it was to the Chinese that the Japanese looked for wisdom. He never reached China, however. On December 3, 1552, Francis died of fever on Sancian (Pinyin Shangchuan) Island, off the coast of Guangdong province, as he attempted to secure entrance to the country that was then closed to foreigners.

ASSESSMENT

Scholarship since the beginning of the 20th century has dispelled many of the legends connected with Xavier and has also defended him against his critics. A modern estimate puts the figure of those baptized by him at about 30,000, as opposed to the 1,000,000 asserted by Baroque exaggeration. In reality he had to struggle with language wherever he worked and did not possess the gift of tongues attributed to him. He is justly credited for his idea that the missionary must adapt to the customs and language of the people he evangelizes, and for his advocation of an educated native clergy—initiatives not always followed by his successors.

Research has shown that he always provided for the continuing pastoral care of the communities he founded and did not abandon them after Baptism as some critics maintained. In fact, many of his own efforts were spent instructing those baptized hastily by others. The areas he evangelized in India have remained Catholic to the present day. Vigorous and prolonged persecution in the 17th century did destroy the missions he founded in the Moluccas and Japan but only after thousands had died as martyrs. Even before his death Francis Xavier was considered a saint, and he has been formally venerated as such by the Catholic Church since 1622. In 1927 he was named patron of all missions.

FRANCISCO VÁZQUEZ DE CORONADO

(b. c. 1510, Salamanca, Spain—d. September 22, 1554, Mexico)

Francisco Vázquez de Coronado was a Spanish explorer of the North American Southwest. His expeditions resulted in the discovery of many physical landmarks, including the Grand Canyon of the Colorado River, but failed to find the fabled treasure-laden cities he sought.

Coronado went to New Spain (Mexico) with Antonio de Mendoza, the Spanish viceroy, in 1535 and earned early distinction in pacifying Indians. He was appointed governor of Nueva Galicia in 1538. Fray Marcos de Niza, sent north in 1539 by Mendoza to explore, had come back with reports of vast riches in the legendary Seven Golden Cities of Cíbola, which perhaps corresponded in reality to the Zuni Pueblos (in present-day New Mexico). Mendoza organized an ambitious expedition to make a more thorough exploration. It consisted of some 300 Spaniards, hundreds of Indians and native slaves, horses, and herds of sheep, pigs, and cattle, in addition to two ships under the command of Hernando de Alarcón, who sailed up the Gulf of California to discover the mouth of the Colorado River on August 26, 1540. In February 1540 the main force under Coronado left Compostela and proceeded up the west coast of Mexico to Culiacán. A smaller unit rode north from there and encountered the Zuni Pueblos in July 1540 but found no great wealth or treasure. Another side exploration made García López de Cárdenas the first European to view the Grand Canyon (in present-day Arizona). The groups united to spend the winter on the Rio Grande at Kuana (near modern Santa Fe, New Mexico). Several Indian groups attempted to attack them there but were beaten back with severe reprisals.

In the spring of 1541, the force moved into Palo Duro Canyon in what is now Texas. There Coronado left most of his men and proceeded north with 30 horsemen to another supposedly fabulously wealthy country, Quivira (Kansas), only to find a seminomadic Indian village and disillusionment again. In 1542 Coronado returned to Mexico, reported his disappointing findings to Mendoza, and resumed his governorship of Nueva Galicia.

Expedition of Francisco Vázquez de Coronado, 1540-42.

An official inquiry, or *residencia*, normally called after an expedition, brought Coronado an indictment for his conduct; but the Mexican *audiencia* (a governing body in the Spanish colonies) found him innocent in February 1546. In his residencia following his governorship he was also indicted, and in this instance he was fined and lost a number of Indians from his landed estate. He retained his seat, however, on the Council of Mexico City until his death.

JUAN RODRÍGUEZ CABRILLO

(d. January 3, 1543?, off the coast of northern California)

Juan Rodríguez Cabrillo (Portuguese: João Rodrigues Cabrilho) was a soldier and explorer in the service of Spain who is chiefly known as the discoverer of California.

Virtually nothing definitive is known of Cabrillo's early life. Although more than one village in Portugal has claimed to be his birthplace, scholars have long debated whether he was of Spanish or Portuguese origin. As a young man, he appears to have accompanied the Spanish conquistador and explorer Pánfilo de Narváez (1520) in his unsuccessful punitive expedition against Hernán Cortés, conqueror of the Aztecs of Mexico. He was evidently one of the conquerors of the region now comprising Guatemala, El Salvador, and Nicaragua. He also may have served for a time as governor of Guatemala. It is thought that Cabrillo embarked from the Mexican port of Navidad in June 1542, explored most of the coast of what is now the state of California, entered San Diego and Monterey bays, and landed on several of the islands near the California coast. He apparently died of complications from a broken leg suffered on one such landing.

CONCLUSION

With the notable exception of individuals such as China's Zheng He, essentially all overseas exploration between the early 15th and the mid-16th centuries was undertaken by Europeans. By 1400 new maritime nations on the Atlantic shores of Europe—such as Spain, Portugal, and England—were growing in economic and military power, and they were now ready to seek overseas trade and adventure. The lure of the East had been felt in Europe since ancient times, as Western traders had reached Southeast Asia and possibly southern China by the 1st century BCE, and some intrepid European adventurers had undertaken the arduous overland journey in the intervening centuries prior to 1400. Marco Polo's book *Il milione* had become immensely popular and had been translated before 1500 from the original Franco-Italian into Latin, German, and Spanish.

Christopher Columbus possessed an annotated copy of the Latin edition (1483–85) of *Il milione*, and in his journal Columbus identified many of his own discoveries with places that Polo had described. The image of the world that Columbus and his contemporaries had was flawed, however, shaped by maps created by the mathematician and astronomer Ptolemy more than 1,200 years earlier. Ptolemy had exaggerated the relative size of the Mediterranean Sea and of Europe and Asia far more than their true extent and had calculated that the vast Indian Ocean was little more than an enclosed inland sea. Nevertheless, the maps provided enough information to give ambitious explorers a chance of success.

Thus, with Ptolemy in one hand and Marco Polo in the other, the European explorers of the Age of Discovery set forth to try to reach the East by new ways. Ptolemy promised that the way was short; Marco Polo promised that the reward was great. It was new routes rather than new lands that filled the minds of kings and commoners, scholars and seafarers. In the process, however, the great navigators of the age happened upon what they gradually came to realize was an entirely New World. The voyages of Columbus westward were soon followed by those of da Gama eastward to India. The circumnavigation of the globe by Magellan and his crew perhaps can be considered the end of the Age of Exploration, although much discovery continued after that, including attempts to find "northern passages" between the Atlantic and Pacific oceans that were shorter and less dangerous routes than the two southern capes. In any event, those many epic voyages paved the way for the emergence of the modern world.

GLOSSARY

adelantado A civil and military governor of a province in Spain or her colonies.

alcalde The chief administrative and judicial officer or the mayor of a town in a Spanish-speaking country or region.

antipodean Situated at the opposite side of Earth.

brigantine A two-masted sailing ship that is square-rigged except for a fore-and-aft mainsail.

cacique A native Indian chief in areas dominated primarily by a Spanish culture.

caravel A small 15th- and 16th-century ship that has broad bows, high narrow poop, and usually three masts with lateen or both square and lateen sails.

conquistador A leader in the Spanish conquest of America and especially of Mexico and Peru in the 16th century.

cordillera A system of mountain ranges often consisting of a number of more or less parallel chains.

corsair Pirate, especially a privateer of the Barbary Coast.

depredation An act of plundering, despoiling, or making inroads.

dom Used as a title prefixed to the Christian name of a Portuguese or Brazilian man of rank.

ducal Of or relating to a duke or dukedom.

eschatological Of or relating to the end of the world.

flotilla A fleet of ships or boats.

garrison A military post or a permanent military installation; also the troops stationed at a garrison.

gonfalonier The chief magistrate or other official of any of several republics in medieval Italy.

ḥājjī One who has made a pilgrimage to Mecca.

hegemony Preponderant influence or authority.

hidalgo In Spain, a hereditary noble or, in the later Middle Ages and the modern era, a knight or member of the gentry.

humanist A Renaissance scholar devoting himself or herself to the study of classical letters.

importunate Overly persistent in request or demand.

infidel An unbeliever with respect to a particular religion.

Inquisition An ecclesiastical tribunal set up in Spain under state control in 1478-80 with the object of proceeding against lapsed converts from Judaism, crypto-Jews, and other apostates that was marked by the extreme severity of its proceedings.

internecine Of, relating to, or involving conflict within a group.

knight-errantry The practice or actions of a knight traveling in search of adventures in which to exhibit military skill, prowess, and generosity.

maravedi An old Moorish gold dinar of Spain and Morocco.

Marrano A Christianized Jew or Moor of medieval Spain.

master of the horse An officer of a prince or noble charged with the care of horses.

mercantile Of or relating to merchants or trading.

merchant marine The privately or publicly owned commercial ships of a nation.

Mishnah The oldest authoritative postbiblical collection and codification of Jewish oral laws, systematically compiled by numerous scholars over a period of about two centuries.

Moorish Of or relating to a Moroccan or, formerly, a member of the Muslim population of what is now Spain and Portugal.

Order of Christ A military order that was started in Portugal after the Knights Templar had been suppressed and that funded a number of exploratory voyages.

Order of Santiago (Portuguese: Order of São Tiago) Christian military-religious order of knights founded about 1160 in Spain for the purpose of fighting Spanish Muslims and of protecting pilgrims on their way to the shrine of Santiago de Compostela.

padrão Stone pillar used by Portuguese explorers to claim land for Portugal.

paleodemography The study of settlement, reproductive, mortality, and other patterns in ancient and prehistoric populations.

paleopathology The study of diseases of former times as evidenced especially in fossil or other remains.

planisphere A polar projection of the celestial sphere and the stars on a plane with adjustable circles or other appendages for showing celestial phenomena for any given time.

portolan A medieval navigation manual illustrated with charts.

reconnoitre To make an exploratory or preliminary survey, inspection, or examination of.

repartimiento In colonial Spanish America, a system by which the crown allowed certain colonists to recruit Indians for forced labour.

residencia A court or inquiry held in Spanish countries for a period of 70 days by a specially commissioned judge to examine into the conduct of a retiring high official (as a viceroy, captain general, governor).

romance A medieval tale based on legend, chivalric love and adventure, or the supernatural.

senhor Lord (a title of nobility).

shipworm Any of various marine clams that cause damage to wharf piles and wooden ships.

subaltern A person holding a subordinate position.

Templar Member of a religious military order of knighthood established at the time of the Crusades that was originally founded to protect Christian pilgrims to the Holy Land and assumed greater military duties during the 12th century.

tributary trade System in China, which for centuries required anyone wishing to trade and deal with China to admit China's cultural and material superiority to all other nations and to come as vassals with tribute (e.g., money or goods) for the emperor.

trumpery Trivial or useless articles.

viceroy The governor of a country or province who rules as the representative of a king or sovereign.

westerly A wind from the west.

zamorin The Hindu sovereign of Calicut and surrounding territory.

BIBLIOGRAPHY

General works discussing aspects of the Age of Exploration include Ronald W. Fritze, *New Worlds: The Great Voyages of Discovery 1400–1600* (2003); Peter C. Muncall (ed.), *Travel Narratives from the Age of Discovery: An Anthology* (2006); and the older but highly comprehensive Samuel Eliot Morison, *The European Discovery of America: The Northern Voyages A.D. 500–1600* (1971, reissued 1993), and *The European Discovery of America: The Southern Voyages A.D. 1492–1616* (1974, reissued 1993).

The 600th anniversary of the start of Zheng He's journeys prompted studies such as Ming-yang Su, *Seven Epic Voyages of Zheng He in Ming China, 1405–1433* (2005); and Fang Zhongfu and Li Erhe, *Peace Missions on a Grand Scale: Admiral Zheng He's Seven Expeditions to the Western Oceans* (2005). P.E. Russell, *Prince Henry the Navigator* (1960, reissued 2001), is a thorough treatment that focuses on his actions as a sponsor of explorations; and Eric Axelson (ed.), *Dias and His Successors* (1988), continues the discussion to those sent in the name of Portugal under the auspices of John II. James A. Williamson, *The Cabot Voyages and Bristol Discovery Under Henry VII* (1962, reprinted 1986), covers the early explorations undertaken for England by John and Sebastian Cabot.

Among works on Christopher Columbus that appeared around the quincentenary of his first voyage are W. Phillips and C.R. Phillips, *The Worlds of Christopher Columbus* (1992); and the outstanding Felipe Fernández-Armesto, *Columbus* (1991), who also wrote *Amerigo: The Man Who Gave His Name to America* (2007), about

Vespucci, Columbus's contemporary and friend. *The Christopher Columbus Encyclopedia, 2 vol.* (1992), is a useful reference work; and Fernando Colón, *The Life of the Admiral Christopher Columbus*, trans. by Benjamin Keen, 2nd ed. (1992), is by Columbus's son. Vespucci's writings are presented in Luciano Formisano (ed.), *Letters from a New World: Amerigo Vespucci's Discovery of America*, trans. by David Jacobson (1992).

Francisco Alvares, *The Prester John of the Indies*, rev. and ed. by G.F. Beckingham and G.W.B. Huntingford, 2 vol. (1961, reissued 2 vol. in 1, 1975), is a narrative of the Portuguese embassy headed by Pêro da Covilhã to Ethiopia in the 1520s. Geneviève Bouchon, *Vasco da Gama* (1997); and Sanjay Subrahmanyam, *The Career and Legend of Vasco da Gama* (1997), are well-written biographies. Antonio Pigafetta, one of the few who sailed with Magellan and returned to Spain, recounts the journey in *The First Voyage Around the World, 1519–1522: An Account of Magellan's Expedition*, ed. by T.J. Cachey (2007); and Laurence Bergreen, *Over the Edge of the World: Magellan's Terrifying Circumnavigation of the Globe* (2003), is both detailed and readable.

Robert H. Fuson, *Juan Ponce de Léon and the Spanish Discovery of Puerto Rico and Florida* (2000), is a comprehensive treatment. Walter Lord (ed.), *Balboa: Discoverer of the Pacific* (1964); and Kathleen Romoli, *Balboa of Darién: Discoverer of the Pacific* (1953), are standard biographies. William H. Prescot, *History of the Conquest of Peru, 2 vol.* (1847); and Clements R. Markham, *A History of Peru* (1892), are two classic accounts of the Pizarro brothers' exploits that have been reissued in many editions since their original publication; and Diego de Castro Tito Cusi Yupanqui, *History of How the Spaniards Arrived in Peru* (2006), is a more recent study. The exploits of the conquistador Cortés are surveyed in Jon Manchip White, *Cortés and the Downfall of the Aztec Empire: A Study in a Conflict of Cultures* (1971, reissued 1989); and William Weber Johnson, *Cortés* (1975, reprinted 1987).

The journals of Cartier's journeys, in original and translation, were edited by H.P. Biggar, *The Voyages of Jacques Cartier* (1924; reissued 1993). Accounts of de Soto's North American expeditions include Charles Hudson, *Knights of Spain, Warriors of the Sun: Hernando de Soto and the South's Ancient Chiefdoms* (1997); and Patricia Galloway (ed.), *The Hernando de Soto Expedition* (1997). Georg Schurhammer, *Francis Xavier: His Life and Times* (1973; originally published in German, 1955–71), is the definitive biography of the renowned proselytizer. George Parker Winship (trans. and ed.), *The Journey of Coronado, 1540–1542* (1904, reissued 1969), is a compilation of firsthand reports of Coronado's exploration of the North American Southwest.

INDEX